Information Security – Risk Management Framework:
For Social Engineering Attacks and Digital Prevention Techniques

Dr. Shekh Abdullah-Al-Musa Ahmed

Information Security
– Risk Management Framework:
For Social Engineering Attacks and Digital Prevention Techniques

Dr. Shekh Abdullah-Al-Musa Ahmed

Academica Press
Washington~London

Library of Congress Cataloging-in-Publication Data
Names: Ahmed, Shekh Abdullah-Al-Musa (author)
Title: Information security – risk management framework : for social engineering attacks and digital prevention techniques | Ahmed, Shekh Abdullah-Al-Musa.
Description: Washington : Academica Press, 2025. | Includes references.
Identifiers: LCCN 2024944093 | ISBN 9781680534238 (hardcover) | 9781680534245 (e-book)

About the Author

Dr. Shekh Abdullah-Al-Musa Ahmed is Assistant Professor in the Department of Computing and Information System at Daffodil International University (DIU). Before joining DIU, he was Assistant Professor in the Faculty of Information and Communication Technology and Department of Computer and Communication Technology at Universiti Tunku Abdul Rahman (UTAR), in Malaysia. He has also worked at Bangladesh University of Business and Technology (BUBT) and Stamford University, Bangladesh. Dr. Ahmed obtained his B.Sc (Hons.) in Computing from UCSI University, Malaysia, a master's degree in Engineering in Information System Security from Bangladesh University of Professionals (BUP), and his doctorate from University Malaysia Kelantan (UMK). He has published frequently on cyber security, IT risk management, and educational research. He has received various recognitions and awards in research and innovation competitions at the national and international levels.

About the Technical Editor

Assoc. Prof. Ts. Dr. Nik Zulkarnaen Khidzir. He is a Certified MBOT Professional Technologist; Associate Professor, Faculty of Creative Technology and Heritage. Currently is a Deputy Director of University Malaysia Kelantan (UMK) International. He is also a member of Technology Advisory Board for Bayarcash, digital financial merchant payment gateway online solution owned by Web Impian Sdn Bhd. In his spare time, he moderates the book "Information Security Risk Management Framework for Social Engineering Attack and Digital Prevention Techniques."

The Author Dedicated this book to the Poet and Lyricist
Sheikh Rana

Preface

In today's digital age, where information preservation is the cornerstone for security and communication, safeguarding this invaluable asset has never been more critical. This book is designed to serve as a dedicated framework for prevention techniques and to navigate the complex and ever evolving landscape of digital data protectionfrom social engineering attacks. It is imperative to recognize the profound significance of role as an information security risk management framework. Every bit and byte of Digital information holds immense value, whether it pertains to personal identities, corporate secrets,or the intellectual property of nations. However, with this value comes vulnerability. In a world rife with cyber threats ranging from sophisticated malware to social engineering tactics, the protection of digital data is not merely a priority—it is an imperative.

This is not only a book on information security and risk management, but a comprehensive compendium meticulously crafted to empower individuals and organizations with the knowledge, tools, and strategies necessary to defend against a multitude of cyber threats. Throughout these pages, the author embarks on multifaceted exploration, beginning with a deep dive into the very essence of digital data protection from social engineering attacks. From understanding the diverse types and classifications of digital information to unravel the intricate web of legal and regulatory frameworks governing data protection, each chapter of this book is meticulously structured to provide a holistic understanding of the subject matter. The establishment of a risk management framework for social engineering attacks does not end there. I hope to transcend theoretical discourse, offering a hybrid method to build a risk management framework. Practical insights drawn from real-world examples, and interviews with industry luminaries. Whether a seasoned cybersecurity professional is seeking to enhance expertise or a novice grappling with the complexities of digital data protection, this book is tailored to meet academician and professional needs. As discussed in the sections, will confront emerging technologies, trends, and threats that shape the cybersecurity landscape. The author will peer into the future, envisioning the innovations and challenges that lie ahead, while equipping with the foresight and resilience needed to stay ahead of the curve. Ultimately, this book is a call to action for people to embrace responsibility as stewards of digital information, to uphold the principles of integrity, confidentiality, and availability in an increasingly interconnected world. The embark on this journey to safeguard our digital future, ensuring that the data entrusted to our care remain secure, resilient, and untarnished by the specter of cyber threats.

Your comprehensive academic guide to digital data protection awaits.

Contents

List of Tables

List Of Figures

Chapter One

Foundations of Information Security risk management: Understanding of social engineering attacks

1.1. Overview of Information Security risk management

Social Engineering is a domain of study in the area of information security. However, every organization currently has its own strategy to protect its own data. On the other hand, social engineering addresses the targeting of humans and machines or technology. This method is popular because human elements are frequently the weakest part of a system and are most prone to mistakes. Human factors cause the security system to start and stop. Weakening of the system occurs when the element fails. The defense actually represents how the end user usually works, and in many cases, the major factor may cause a catastrophic impact on the organization due to the lack of awareness and knowledge of the end user. This result shows the insecurity of an organizational environment.

A reactive or proactive approach might involve human factors, where security incidents and system termination may cause problems before they become problems. The role of an information security specialist is to increase awareness of SoE attack risks among employees and to provide brief descriptions of SoE attack risks, such as threats, vulnerabilities, management defects, unexpected changes and digital evidence factors. This is evidence that social engineering is a very basic level of attack. Once the malicious person obtains information from the target victim, the attack is started. According to the survey, approximately 88% of clicking links within email were reported to phishing. Whereas most common phishing attacks occurring at financial institutes. However, it is difficult to estimate how much email is sent every day. However, 65% of emails consist of malware. Specifically, previous studies emphasize that social engineering is a kind of art that helps people to reveal confidential digital evidence.

Thus, even though business continuity concepts are widely recognized within organizations, with the success of integrating the prevention technique of social engineering attack risks and SoE attack risk management practices. Hence, this study attempts to develop an information security risk management framework for the prevention of social engineering attacks. An appropriate risk management process and activities can manage social engineering risks in the information security domain. A literature review reveals the impact of social engineering attacks in various sectors. However, analysis of the risk of the SoE attacking, data security and protection has revealed a lack of business continuity knowledge, lack of disaster recovery planning, and disturbance of organizational productivity. This is the reason for social engineering attack risks. Surveys need to be conducted to determine the impact of these attacks on the organization. Social engineering risks can be described as threats, vulnerabilities, management defects, unexpected changes and digital evidence factors in the organization. However, every organization is connected to an internet database server.

Hence, vulnerability reflects the weakness of the system. Threats express how to exploit this weakness of the system, management defects show the management weakness of the organization, and unexpected changes show the lack of awareness inside the organization. Digital evidence indicates essential or sensitive information that SoE attackers are interested in collecting from the organization. However, different organizations have different impacts from social engineering attacks. Subsequently, a dedicated information security framework could be used to address and manage the mitigation of social engineering risk. Hence, risk management practices for preventing SoE attack risk include an organization's approach to maintaining the confidentiality, availability, integrity, nonrepudiation, accountability, authenticity and reliability of its systems. Information Security Risks, IT risks, IT related risks, and internet risks are risk types that are related to SoE attack risks in the domain of information security. Digital evidence is a valuable and important property or asset, and the SoE attack risk management leads organizations to become increasingly dependent on adopting a security framework. Various social engineering attacks may occur inside an organization, which can disturb personal productivity. Hence, this approach involves identifying the problem, the relevant questions and the objectives that were determined for creating the framework. A suitable methodology and various analysis techniques were then designed to achieve the objectives.

The banking sector began to become aware of any kind of information security attack, such as social engineering attack. After that, other local banks implemented the protection of assets against information security attacks or any kind of critical or disaster situations. Some other Banks started initiative regarding the protection against any kind of social engineering attack in the banking system. Subsequently, other organizations began to practice awareness of social engineering attacks in an attempt to give more focus to their core business. Together, these findings support the development of a framework for preventing SoE attacks. However, the term digital evidence refers to evidence that is available in binary numbers such as 0 or 1. Digital evidence is confined to evidence produced by digital technology.

The broad nature of the internet has allowed the social engineering crimes worldwide. Therefore, it is important to have a framework for the prevention of social engineering attacks and proper management of such attacks. Proper risk management approaches in various organizations could lead to successful proper implementation. Previous research has been conducted to provide evidence that incorporating social engineering attack risks can improve the success of framework implementation and reduce the catastrophic events. While other studies have focused on information security risk, the management of social engineering attack risk has not been explored.

Thus, there are still significant gaps in knowledge that need to be investigated to develop a robust understanding of such social engineering attack risks, leading to a comprehensive approach to risk management for healthcare centers, education, government agencies and the banking sector. To meet the objectives of the present research, a mixed method technique was applied. The use of quantitative research methods establishes purposiveness, rigor, testability, explication, precision and confidence, objectivity, generalizability and parsimony. Moreover, the qualitative research method allows for in-depth and detailed exploration.

In fact, an information system is a unit that includes people, processes and systems. There are numerous risks that organizations must handle, and these can have catastrophic outcomes on the continuing future of the organization. In the previous few years, a proliferation of automatic information systems, reliance on the internet to permit all of the fundamental service and infrastructures and the growing risk of organizing social engineering attacks with the capability of creating debilitated disruptions of organizational digital evidence. The proliferation of computer systems and the growth of the internet have empowered not only novel services but also new services. For example, email, websites and electronic digital commerce have positive impacts on organizations, allowing them to run businesses with reputations.

Hence, information and communication technology has the potential to increase the risk of social engineering attacks. However, the SoE attack risks associated with SoE attack risk management practices theory must be evaluated and managed. Therefore, an awareness program is required for SoE attacks because the technology can cause problems due to malicious human activity.

Hence, a variety of standard frameworks have been developed to address multiple business operations and specific technical processes. Therefore, there is a need for organizations to formulate an appropriate framework to secure digital evidence to support continuous business operation. However, there are several established risk management and analysis approaches for information security risk management, such as OCTAVE, CORA, and the IS Business Model, has been developed around the globe. Unfortunately, very little research has been conducted on social engineering attack risk and on how risk management practices prevent SoE attacks in various organizations. However, the risk management approaches comprehensively guide practitioners and how to manage information security risk in the context of social engineering attack risk-based solutions.

1.2. Aims and Objectives

The overall aim of this study is to develop an information security risk management framework for the prevention technique of social engineering attacks that can assist organizations in managing to reduced social engineering attack risks.

Specifically, the objectives of the study are as follows:

1. To identify various SoE attack risks.
2. To analyze SoE attack risks in various organizations.
3. The purpose of this study was to integrate SoE attack risks with risk management practices forthe prevention of SoE attacks.
4. To develop an information security risk management framework for preventing SoE attacksthrough expert judgment.

Table 1.1: Objectives, questions and analysis

Study Objective	Study Question	Study Analysis
Objective 1: To identify various SoEattacking risks.	Q1 What is the results for descriptive analysis of thestudy?	Exploratory study.
Objective 2: To analyze SoE attacking risks in various organization.	Q1. What are the ranking of critical SoE attacking risks items in the organizations? Q2. What are the significant characteristics associated with attacking risks in the organizations? Q3. What are the relationship of SoE attacking risk with Organizational Activities?	Empirical approach of study. Furthermore, empirical analysis such as assessment measurement model and assessment structural model done on the framework.
Objective 3: To integrate SoE attacking risks with riskmanagement practice for the prevention technique of SoE attacks.	Q1. What are the component of SoE attacking risk management? Q2. What are the relationship of risk management practice with Organizational Activities?	Exploratory approach of research study.
Objective 4: To develop information security risk management framework for the prevention technique of SoE attacks through expert judgment.	Q1. What is the results of confirmatory study? Q2. How do the result of the expert judgment support the suitability and applicability of the proposed framework?	Expert judgment approach and technique for the confirmatory study.

1.3. Significance of the work

The activity provides empirical data for social engineering risks in the organization. These findings are useful for understanding organizational perceptions of SoE attack risks. These activities also provide exploratory data for SoE attack risk management practices in organizations, and an information security risk management framework is finally proposed for preventing SoE attacks. Understanding the social engineering attack risk construct and its implications will further enhance decision-making guidelines for prevention measurement approaches to ensure its successful deployment.

A prior activity showed that SoE attack risk management practices contribute to reduced SoE attack risk in various organizations, and a closer analysis of these risks and their management practices will assist organizations in further improving the process of identifying and analyzing, planning and managing SoE attack risks. Fundamentally, the findings from the organization clarify that the impact is valuable if any kind of SoE attack risk occurs in the organization. However, these attacks can cause disturbances in natural productivity. Moreover, the study provided a list of SoE attack risk items that are represented in perspective, some of which had never raised the attention of other frameworks.

Finally, the information security risk management framework for preventing SoE attacks proposed in this study could be used as a point of reference and to provide guidelines for managing social engineering risks in various organizations.

1.4. Novelty of the work

This activity extends the existing work on SoE attack risk areas in the domain of information security, capabilities and strategies. First, specific empirical studies on social engineering attack risks and SoE attack risk management practices and this type of work have never been conducted before. While previous activities have identified and classified the major SoE attack risks in this field, the broader question of how these challenges should be managed, has yet to be answered. Furthermore, few researchers have investigated the relationship between SoE attack risks and risk management practices for preventing SoE attacks in organizations.

In addition, previous studies have typically examined SoE attack risks in information and communication technology and SoE attack risk management. There is also limited work thus that has investigated the level of security of digital evidence in organizations. Additionally, the in activity has identified new SoE attack risks as realized by information security professionals or experts. These new SoE attack risks contributed to the originality of the study.

A dedicated framework was introduced to manage the prevention technique of SoE attack risks in various organizations to further the existing work in this area. There are limited numbers of researchers who have focused on comprehensive and structured guidelines for managing SoE attack risks in various sectors. This in activity focuses on the specific information security risk management framework for the prevention technique of SoE attacks in the organization to reap the full benefits of improving the information security process.

1.5. Contribution to the society

The study has significant empirical, academic and managerial contributions. From the managerial perspective, the findings contribute to improving the way an organization manages SoE attack risks in various organizations. This was made possible by the discovery of the SoE attack risks that influence the practices of SoE risk management for various organizations. This finding also provides insight into how organizations practice the prevention technique of SoE attack risk management, thus contributing to their academic and managerial contributions.

Moreover, the findings provide empirical support for establishing the relationship between SoE risks and risk management practices for preventing SoE attacks. The risks of SoE attacks have been identified from the literature review and consequently investigated. This was further substantiated by empirical evidence based on the organization's perceptions regarding SoE attack risks, which have been ranked based on their level of criticalness in various organizations. This part would be the empirical contribution.

However, there has not been much related work on SoE attacking risks for in-house organization implementation and the approach used in managing them, this study extends its managerial and academic contributions by identifying the risk management of SoE attacks that are relevant to the organizational environment. The semi structured approach was used with professional employees to gain insight into emerging SoE attack risks and the appreciation of managing these risks for various organizations.

The main contribution of this work is the development of a risk management framework for the prevention technique of SoE attack risks for various organizations. In addition to being empirically validated through proven statistical analysis methods and exploratory study applications in the organization, the framework is also theoretically supported, thus making the proposed framework reliable for use in the organization as a guide in managing the prevention technique of SoE attack risks.

In most scientific and technological work, two broad approaches are known as deductive and inductive methods. The inductive approach is usually described as it moves from specific to general. On the other hand, the deductive approach begins with the general and ends with the specific. The methodology is commonly described as a systematic process for collecting, analyzing and interpreting data to increase the understanding of phenomena or problems related to the research areas of interest or concern. With respect to scientific methods, the process requires researchers to identify problems, draw hypotheses or set questions to obtain information related to problems, and analyze or interpret data to support or refute questions or hypotheses.

Qualitative, quantitative and mixed or hybrid methods constitute the main methods used. However, the practices of these methods differ among researchers and depend on the questions and their objectives. The qualitative methods emphasize the meaning of definitions, concepts, context, descriptions and environmental settings. The quantitative method focuses on measurement and statistics. However, both methods focus on the importance of objectivity, observation and data collection in conducting work.

For the purpose of this study, both approaches (deductive and inductive) and mixed methods, such as quantitative and qualitative methods, were applied to identify the knowledge gap in the area, answer the related question and fulfill the objectives of the study. Figure 1.1 illustrates the five phases of the methodology used in this study.

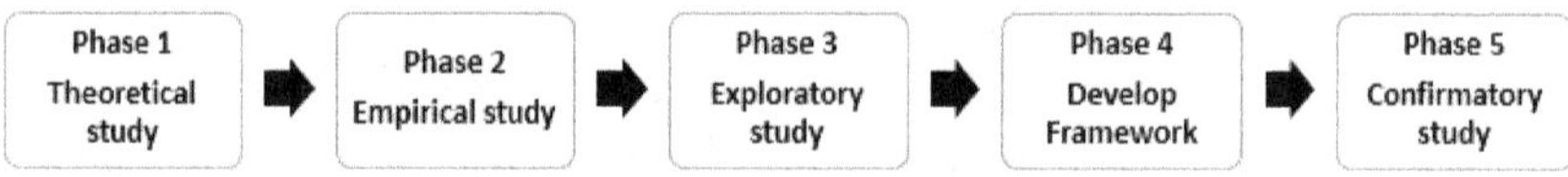

Figure 1.1: Methodology of study

However, better documents for comprehending related areas and identifying existing knowledge gaps. The conceptual study focused on two knowledge areas, SoE attack risks and prevention techniques, such as risk management, which would help to build an information security risk management framework for the prevention technique of SoE attacks. Other related concepts and theories were also reviewed as supplementary support for the conceptual study. The exploratory inputs, research approach and results of the conceptual study phase are illustrated in Figure 1.2.

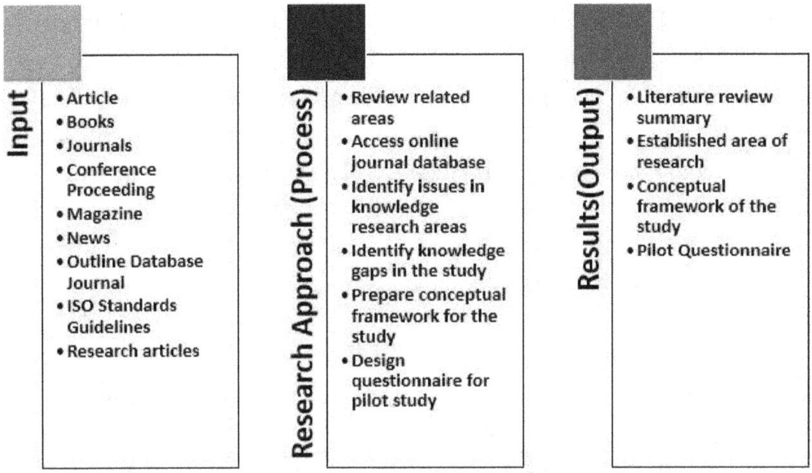

Figure 1.2: Exploration of the inputs, research approach and results of the conceptual study phase

In phase 2, the empirical study phase, the pilot questionnaire was validated through appropriate statistical analysis. Then, to refine the questionnaire suitability for the activity, subject–matter experts (SMEs) verified and validated the questionnaire. The details of the validation process are explained in chapter 3. A refined questionnaire was distributed to investigate the factors that influence the practice of preventing SoE attacks. And to assess the risk management practices of SoE attacks as well as digital evidence security requirement in the organization. The input research approach and results of the empirical study phase are summarized in Figure 1.3.

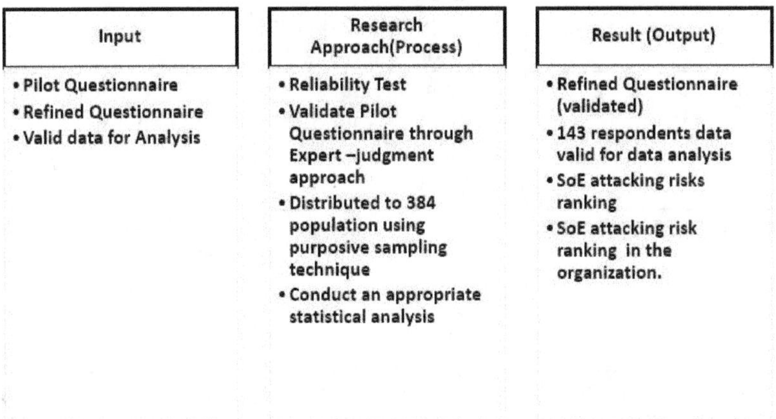

Figure 1.3: Empirical Study Phase Approach

In phase 3, the exploratory study phase, semi structured methods were used with focus groups of eight organizations that were directly involved in SoE awareness implementation. Each focus group consisted of personnel who possessed wide experience in understanding SoE attack risks and risk management practices in the organization. The second part of the exploratory study phase, included a comparison of the findings of the results of the empirical study and literature review. An overview and outputs of the exploratory study phase are illustrated in Table 1.2.

Table 1.2: Exploratory study phase: study approach

Input	Study Approach (process)	Results (output)
Semi structured way was used to focus group	Comparison analysis of the focus group	Confirm existing SoE attacking risk.
Conceptual study results	Identify SoE attacking riskmanagement practice for the prevention technique in the organization.	Prevention technique of SoE attack in the organization and the themeof the risk management process.
Empirical study results	Compare result of focus group with empirical and conceptual study supported with the finding.	Semi structured way was used for the SoE attacking risks in various organizations.
Related documents or reports	Identify similar and contradicting practices from empirical results and exploratory study results.	SoE attacking risk.
Past literature	Integrating the SoE attacking risk with SoE attacking risk management.	High –Level prevention technique for the development of framework.
Current or best practices		Critical analysis of SoE attacking risk managementpractices in the organization.

In phase 4, the framework development phase, the results obtained from the conceptual,empirical and exploratory study phases will be used to develop a framework for the prevention technique of SoE attacks in the organization and the detailed component of the framework. In this phase, related worksheets are also developed to improve the understanding of each component of the framework. A detailed explanation of the inputs, study approach and expected results involved in this phase are provided in Table 1.3

Table 1.3: Framework development phase: Study approach

Input	**Study Approach(process)**	**Results (Output)**
SoE attacking risk factors in the organization	Content analysis of resultsin previous study phases	Refined high-level framework.
Refined High –level framework	Synthesize previous phaseresults	Components of the proposed framework.
Results from previous phases	Develop flow of practices in managing SoE attackingrisks in the organization	Draft of the proposed framework.
	Develop flow and steps in the managing SoE attacking risks in the organization.	Proposed framework user manual
	Develop recommended worksheet that can be usedtogether with the framework.	Recommended related worksheets used in the proposed framework.

In phase 5, a confirmatory study was conducted to test the suitability and applicability of the proposed framework. An expert judgment approach was used in order to verify the acceptability of the framework for the organization and the community. Table 1.4 describes the input, activity and results involved in the confirmatory phase.

Table 1.4: Confirmatory study phase: Study approach

Input	**Study Approach (process)**	**Results (Output)**
Related Documents	Review results of previous phase	Verified framework
Literature articles	Review and compare related documents.	Validated framework

Input	Study Approach (process)	Results (Output)
Proposed framework	Assess past findings	Validated framework byexperts
	In-depth framework validation with experts (expert judgment)	
	Compile results of validation (comments orrecommendations)	

To achieve the stated study objectives and to ensure the reliability of the results. The validity of the findings, consistency of the conclusions, and appropriate methodology techniques for data collection and analysis were used.

The study focus areas and scope are as follows:

1. The study is limited to the organization, identifying the SoE attack risks from top managementpractitioners.
2. The study focused solely on SoE attack risk management practices.
3. The study emphasizes the adoption of the prevention technique of SoE attack risk managementand implementation in organizations.
4. The expert-judgment approach focuses on evaluating the suitability and applicability of theproposed framework that would be implemented in the organization.

The challenges and constraints in conducting this study were as follows:

1. The limited access to confidential secondary data and reports meant that recommendations orsuggestions were based only on the data provided and supported by previous literature.
2. The number of respondents was limited. When a return rate of 143 was deemed sufficient, morerespondents would have produced more accurate results.
3. The semi-structured approach was used during the exploratory study phase, which involvedsetting a time with the focus groups due to their other work commitments.

The study will unfold in the following manner.

Chapter 1 provides an introduction to the scope of the study area, as well as the methodology approach employed.

Chapter 2 introduces the theoretical background and fundamentals of the study and conceptual framework of the work, engaging with and referring to the recent literature in the areas of various organizations, global information security issues and associated SoE attack risks, SoE attack risk management practices in organizations and information security risk management frameworks for the prevention technique of SoE attacks. The content analysis approach was used in the study of these references. The identified practices from the key components for developing the conceptual framework of the study and the subsequent proposed framework for the prevention technique of SoE attacks.

Chapter 3 discusses the study approach and methodology involved in the data collection and data analysis methods. Through purposive sampling, questionnaires were distributed to 384 respondents in various organizations for a return rate of 36%. Moreover, a semi structured method was used with eight focus groups to further clarify some of the findings of the empirical study.

Chapter 4 focuses on the analysis and results using appropriate data analysis techniques. The results of the analysis provided evidence on how organizations practice risk management for the prevention of SoE attacks. These findings could subsequently contribute to developing a framework for preventing SoE attacks in organizations. Hence, we concentrate on an exploratory analysis based on a semi structured approach with focus groups from eight different organizations. Similarly, the findings were used for developing a framework for preventing SoE attack risk in organizations.

Chapter 5 discusses the process of framework development and designing the flow of the proposed framework. This chapter also presents the proposed a framework for preventing SoE attacks in organizations. The detailed framework components, such as the stages, processes and activities, are explained further in this chapter.

Chapter 6 discusses the process of conducting a confirmatory study to validate the framework through expert judgment of this area of risk management involving SoE attacks. This chapter also presents the results of the confirmatory study and verifies the usability and applicability of the proposed framework for the organization. The supplementary finding by discussing the answers to the work question and the fulfillment of the objectives. This also discusses the findings, and provides several recommendations for organizations, information security professionals and decision makers. Finally, the chapter offers some directions for future work.

Chapter Two

"Navigating the Digital Terrain: Understanding Data, Risks, and Regulations"

2.1. Definition of digital data Types of digital data (personal, sensitive, corporate, etc.)

This chapter aims to explore the related theories and concepts in the domain, then examine the SoE attack risk approaches and identify knowledge gaps. A review of the literature in the area of various organizations, as well as the approaches and theoretical lens used in SoE attack risk and SoE attack risk management practices, is conducted to position this work within the studies. This chapter clarifies the viewpoints of SoE attack risks and SoE attack risk management practices in organizations from an interpretative perspective. The fundamental concepts of study were extensively explored. The discussion begins with a review of the various related literature related to the organizations, associated with SoE attack risks, SoE attack risk management practices and methodologies for addressing the prevention technique of SoE attacks. Drawing upon previous studies, the significant knowledge gaps in the field will be identified to develop the context for the study.

Every organization has the act of delegating or transferring information security related decision making rights, business processes, internal activities and services to external providers who develop, manager and administer these activities in accordance with agreed upon deliverables, performance standards and outputs, as set forth in the contractual agreement. Organizations invest in this strategy to reduce any kind of SoE attack risk. The previous literature review revealed forty- four (44) SoE attack risk items, which are most common in organizations. For example, in poor SoE detection studies, disorganized organizational staff, unreliable digital evidence protection, lack of suitable control of digital evidence accessibility, and staff negligence of service providers such as programmers technical tester and manager, lack of business continuity plan management, frequent changes in business policies, legal activity and documentation, organizational policy of employee online information updates, lack of security training and awareness regarding SoE attacks, insufficient attention given to human factors of SoE attacks in design implementation, etc. Since the process and phases in the organizations' information security strategy implementation are similar, the generic process was introduced. The generic services used in the organization are as follows: information protection, selection service provider, contract management and ongoing monitoring. A generic information security cycle is proposed through the adoption of several published works and relevant theories, such as Transaction Cost Theories (TCTs) and agency theories (AT) and rationale exchange theories (RET). Figure 2.1 illustrates the life cycle of generic organizations for information security and relevant theories.

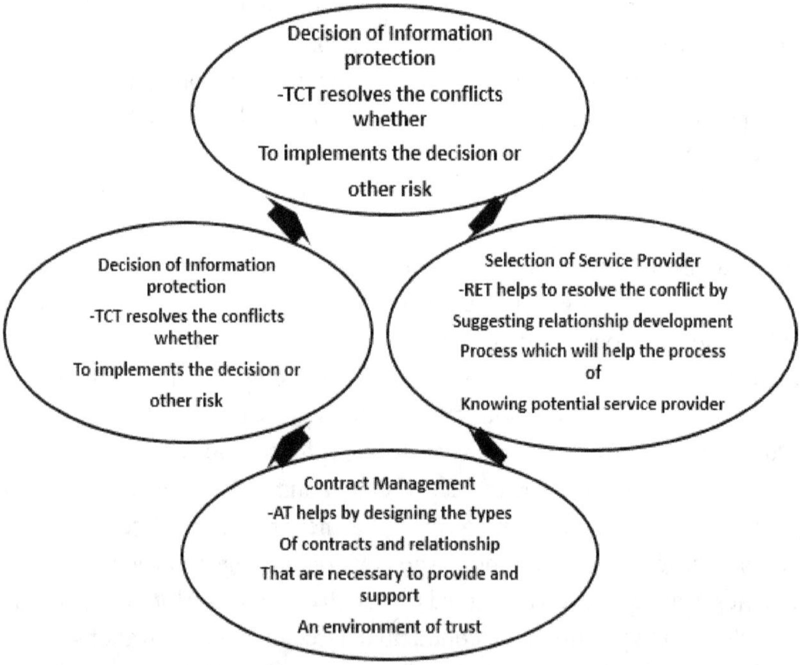

Figure 2.1: Generic information security management in organizations and supported theories

Many organizations are experiencing the fastest growth and evolution of business activities worldwide. Therefore, the term "organizations" encompasses a broad spectrum of technologies, complexities and sizes and takes many forms. The important classes of organizations include contract-manufacturing, facility management, and business process- provisioning processes, namely, human resources, finance, and customer support. Organizations normally call for service providers to cut costs while improving business efficiency by focusing on their core businesses. While the strategy has proven to be effective, it may also bring about significant risks that must be recognized and managed. Beyond this advantage, organizations have approaches with potential risks. However, previous researchers risks into seven types strategic, operational, financial, regulatory or legal compliance, technological risk, reputational risk and SoE attack risk.

Table 2.1: The risk category descriptions and examples are shown

Category	**Description**	**Example**
Strategic risk	Refers to how well organizations have aligned its activities with its overall business strategy and placing the resources and structures in the place to execute them.	Inconsistent with the organization's strategy goals of the regulated entity. Inadequate management experience and expertise can lead to a lack of understanding and control. Inadequate expertise to oversee the service provider.
Operational risk	Refers to the risks of service providers to actually deliver the service to the expected standards, whether that be in terms of quality, quantity or timelines (ability of service provider to response or recover from unforeseen events)	Technological failure.Inability to maintain a competitive position. Fraud or error. Inability to deliver products or services. Inability to manage information.
Financial risk	Financial risks occurs throughout many element of the deal, starting with transition. It is common for surprised to appear during the transition, which can driven up costs for organizations.	Inadequate financial capacity to fulfill obligations and provide remedies. The future unfolding in an unpredicted scenario whereas the pricing mechanism was designed as part of the initial contract.

Category	Description	Example
Regulator or legal Compliance	Risk caused by violation of law, rules, regulations, prescribed, practices, contract and ethical standards.	Privacy are not complied. Service provider has inadequate compliance systems and controls.
Technological Risk	Risks relating to the failure of service providers electronic data processing environment to effectively and surely process and deliver product to the organizations.	Incompatible development tools. Non compliance with embrace methodology. Conflicting development standards.
Reputational Risk	Risks of negative publicity regarding business practice.	Poor reputation of serviceprovider. Service provider practicesnot in line with stated practice of regulated entity.
SoE attacking risk	SoE attacking risks are caused of threat action on vulnerabilities that contribute to SoE attacking risk incidents. The core information security fundamental principles such as confidentiality, integrity and availability are the basis in deterring the risks.	Identify theft and personal data or information. Loss, damage or destruction of digital evidence. SoE who destroy or threaten to destroy digital evidence. Extraction of loss of valuable or private information (Business records and Client'sprofiles)

Other studies also support the view that SoE attack risk is considered to be the most basiclevel ofattack in information security domains, and organizations need to successfully address this risk to ensure maximum benefit and implement strategies to protect digital evidence against suchattacks.

Hence, this significant risk in organizations must ensure the confidentiality, integrity andavailability of digital evidence. Different areas tend to derive different definitions of risk, especially since the term appears in many fields of study. However, the definitions of SoE attacksare unique descriptions, focusing on risk factors that address prevention techniques for SoE attack risk and managing the risks of SoE attack, such as security breaches, physical security, confidentiality issues, information leakage, threats and vulnerability issues. The most cited social engineering attack risk issues in the organization are tabulated in Table 2.2.

Table 2.2: SoE Attacking Risks

SoE Attacking Risks	SoE Attacking Risks Description	References
SoE attacking risks issues	Security breaches, information leakage, physical security, confidentiality issues, integrity and availability issues, threats, vulnerabilities, unexpected change in management, management defects in organization, digitalevidence.	Abdullah, A et al., 2017; Fan et al., 2017; Gewald et al., 2014; Hartini et al., 2013; Ian Mann., 2018; Ana et al., 2016; Ayesha et al., 2013; Bob et al., 2005; Christopher., 2018; Clif A. Ericson., 2016; Cooke et al., 2017; Cooke etal., 2012; Daniel et al., 2016; Edward., 2015; Fan., 2017;Georg., 2014; Hinson G., 2008.

A breach of security occurs when a stated organizational policy or legal requirement regarding information security has been contravened. SoE activities are some kind of art, such as from outside an organization, that bypasses or contravenes security policies. Recent social engineering attacks include phishing, visiting and impersonation. These attacks reveal data security breaches, involving external malicious persons and company insider attackers hence, thistype of activity has increased to extraordinary levels. This finding augments the view that information and data security breaches still constitute the most critical issue of SoE attack risks. In these organizations, external or outsider parties of SoE attackers could be individuals who are directly involved in committing the attack because of their live internet connection and who may become the perpetrators of the source of information security breaches.

Information leakage currently yet another critical threat of SoE attack risk in organizations. Information leakage refers to the accidental or intentional release of information to certain people before it is made available to a general employee. It is recognized as an increasingly significant problem, since computing services have made it much easier for SoE attackers to gain access to organizational employee information related to confidential data. Furthermore, the information leakage can be seen as an indication of the efforts required for a successful attack by SoE attackers and could be used for security risk assessment and security policy compliance decisions.

Physical security is often a discounted discipline, yet attention is given to safeguarding. A physical environment can yield a satisfactory level of protection. A good physical security program is provided in an organization's first line of defense to secure valuable digital evidence. Therefore, organizations should pay more attention to safeguarding their physical environment for their business continuity since they involve external parties. Physical security allows more control over service providers access to organizational information and physical access to organizations information and physical assets, such as physical computer facilities. It includes access to buildings, to the computer room(s), to the computers (mainframe, mini, micros), to the magnetic media, and to other media. Biometric devices record physical traits (such as fingerprints, palm prints, facial features, etc) or behavioral traits (signatures, typing habits, etc.). Unauthorized access to these facilities is also considered an SoE attack risk that could lead to risk in the organization.

Other significant SoE attack risk issues need to be considered during the implementation of organizational SoE attack risk of threats, the SoE attack risk of vulnerabilities, the SoE attack risk of management defects, the SoE attack risk of unexpected changes and the SoE attack risk of digital evidence. These risk factors for SoE attacks could directly involve organizational digital evidence and contribute to risk incidents of SoE attacks. Researchers have highlighted several threats and vulnerabilities, management defects, unexpected changes and digital evidence as SoE attack risks. However, there is still a need for further research on this risk category to explore the real SoE attack risks involved when organizations continue their business.

2.2. Fundamentals of Digital Evidence

Social engineering attacks, are is one kind of criminal proceeding. In addition, the wrong or digital crime can be determined, and the offender can be punished. To achieve the legal system through the machineries of administration of justice and the main agents of these machineries are the courts of lawyers. However, it is a major challenge to the court or lawyers to prove the existence of rights, liabilities or digital crime. This is where the importance of the law of digital evidence lies. However, digital evidence is described as computer print or output and is admissible in court.

Generally, the criminal proceeding has the following four stages:

-Preprocessing Stage (Police and Investigation Officers)
-Proceeding Stage (Court)
-Trial stage (court)

-Post trial Stage (Police or Jail authority)

In the initial stages of malicious social engineering personnel activity and the investigation of criminal activity and the preparation of criminal cases, the police and information security investigator officers' role from the beginning to the end of this end stage would be very crucial. This stage has the following sub- heads: -

-FIRs in cognizable offences
-Complaint in no cognizable and cognizable offenses.
-Reporting to the Magistrate.
-Investigating malicious person SoE activity and maintaining case Diary.
-Final Report / Charge sheet

Hardware, software, data or information, people and services are the five relevant assets groups in organizations. Hence, data or information assets are the only digital evidence type associated with information security domains. Close analysis has shown that the success of organizational functions depends on a complex set of requirements that also involve the protection of digital evidence. However, digital evidence refers to a collection of facts in the form of paper or electronic messages, content. Subject matter and substance forms can be used to draw conclusions to meet the missions and objectives of organizations. In summary, digital evidence could be the best term for representing any knowledge or data term that is of value to the organization. Some examples of digital evidence include systems documentation, operational procedures, business records, client profiles, databases, data files, and training materials. The continuity plan, fallback arrangements and archived information were used.

In recent years, the importance of digital evidence as a key asset has continued to grow, since its production, complexity, volume and demand accelerated. However, the fulfillment of real digital evidence needs has been limited due to various obstacles. Especially in organizations, one such obstacle is inappropriate classification. The classification of digital evidence concerns its confidentiality, integrity and availability. Hence, anything occurring with three CIAs would cause the SoE to attack digital evidence at risk. To date, only limited numbers of researchers have focused on classifying digital evidence according to the security requirements of organizations. Therefore, it is important to consider ensuring secure digital evidence in organizations.

Several different digital evidence characteristics are described in the ISO/IEC 27000 Standards Series (ISO/IEC 27000:2018) and are commonly used in the information security domain, such as the SoE attack risk management system. These characteristics were also well documented in digital evidence inventories and register documents (ISO/IEC 27000:2018, ISO27K Implement's Forum, 2017). Digital data such as personal and financial, legal databases, digital archives, etc. Tangible digital evidence (such as research and development, strategic and commercial, journal, books, etc.), intangible digital evidence (such as knowledge, business relationships, licenses, patents, trademarks, accumulated experience, reputation, customer confidence, etc.); application software (such as client software, computing desktop application, e-business application, etc.), IT hardware assets (such as storage devices, modems and line terminators, communication devices, etc.) and IT service assets (such as user authentication and administration processes, hyperlinks, firewalls, wireless services, IDS and IPS, etc.) from the significant information assets characteristics used to present as digital evidence in the organizations. Various types of digital evidence are involved in organizational activities before starting any kind of business activity. The fourteen common digital records in the organizations identified from the literature, include business and financial records, client profiles, business continuity plans, archived data or information, policy and procedure documents, financial proposal documents, technical proposal documents, solution requirement specifications, business requirement architecture, system documentation, electronic files and contract documents and database and data files. Table 2.3 highlights the relevant digital evidence in the organization and its nature.

Table 2.3: Digital evidence in the organization

Common digital evidence	Digital evidence characteristics
Business and financial Records	Digital data, Intangible, IT hardware, Application software.
Client's profiles	Digital data, Intangible
Business Continuity plan	Digital data, Tangible or Intangible
Archived Data or Information	Digital data, Tangible, ApplicationSoftware
Policy and procedures	Digital data, Tangible Intangible

Common digital evidence	Digital evidence characteristics
Business Requirements Architecture	Digital data, Tangible
System Documentation	Digital data, Tangible
Electronic Files and Records	Digital data, tangible, ApplicationSoftware, IT Services asset
Training material of SoE attacksawareness	Digital data, Tangible
Legal and contract Documents	Digital data, Tangible
Database and data files	Digital data, Tangible, Applicationsoftware.
Financial Proposal Documents	Digital data, Tangible
Technical proposal Documents	Digital data, Tangible
Solution Requirement Specifications	Digital data, Tangible

Sources: Sundresan Perumal., 2009; Siti et al., 2008; Manes et al., 2010; Gita Radhakrisna., 2014;Suci et al., 2017.

2.3. SoE Attacking Risks

A malicious person will look for targets of opportunity for organizational digital evidence. SoE attack risks include threats or vulnerabilities that contribute to SoE attack risk incidents. Common SoE attack risks of thefts include personal data on information leakage and unauthorized exploration of intellectual property (IP). These information security risks are caused by a lack of control in the organization. However, the risk of threats being attacked by SoE refers to finding the weakness of the system to explore organizational digital evidence. In addition to other kinds of SoE attacks, threats such as fraudsters organized crimes such as phishing emails and unwanted phone calls, unauthorized access and malware authors are actors or situations that might deliberately or accidently exploit threats and that could be the cause of SoE attacks. The literature identifies ten (10) most frequent SoE attack risks of threat items in organizations. Table 2.4 describes the ten (10) SoE attack risks of threat items used for the study.

Table 2.4: Literature review of the risk of SoE attacking threat items

SoE attacking risks of threats item	Literature References
Poor social engineering attack detection studies.	Algarni et al., 2017; Hinson G, 2012; Jean Boltz., 2015.
Directly exploit control weakness in the systems.	Hinson. G., 2016; Nik. Z. et al, 2018; Jean Boltz., 2015.
Exploit other control weakness involving printed or other information rather than computer data and system.	Hinson. G., 2008; Todd. F.,2016.
Unauthorized access to or modification or disclosure of digital evidence	Nik. Z. et al, 2018; Jean Boltz., 2015.
Information leakage (extraction of loss of valuable or private information)	Louis. A., 2010; Jean Boltz., 2015.
Unauthorized exploitation of intellectual property (IP)(example : plagiarism, etc.)	Noor. H. et al., 2007; Peltier. T. R., 2012.
Widespread unauthorized and uncontrolled used of portable devise andtransportable computer media.	Rahul Singh., 2015; Jean Boltz., 2015.
Identify theft of personal data or Information.	Rahul Singh., 2015; Nik. Z. et al, 2014.
System error and failures	Rai Kaplan., 2005; Sandelowski. M., 2013.
Loss, damage or destruction of digital evidence in the organization.	Suit & Han., 2008; Tim. M et al., 2015.

Another key element that contributes to SoE attack risks is vulnerability. Vulnerabilities refer to the weaknesses of a safeguard in an asset that make a threat potentially more harmful (can be exploited), more likely to occur, or more likely to occur more frequently. There are twelve (12) common SoE attack risks of vulnerabilities identified from the literature. Vulnerabilities such as user system accounts are not used; insufficient backup, disorganized organizational staff, complex information technology and systems; and lack of asset inventory management. Table describes the twelve (12) The SoE attack risk of vulnerabilities identified from various literature reviews used in this study.

Table 2.5: Literature review of the risk of SoE attacking vulnerabilities

SoE attacking risks of vulnerabilities item	Literature references
User system accounts not is use.	Nina Godbole., 2017; Rahul Singh., 2015; Noor. H. et al, 2010.
Insufficient backup.	Nina Godbole 2017; Jean Boltz., 2015.
Disgruntled of organizational staff.	Mohamed, N & Zakaria., 2013; Mark Merkow etal., 2015.
Complexity of information technology and system.	Nina Godbole 2017; Katharina. K. et al., 2015.
Lack of assets inventory management.	Jean Boltz., 2015; K.Papadaki., 2015.
Unreliable level of digital evidenceprotection.	Jeb. W. et al., 2015.
Inadequate investment in appropriateSoE attacking risk control.	Todd. F., 2016; Hinson. G., 2013.
Lack of suitable control of digitalevidence accessibility.	Dwyer. F., et al., 1999.
Inadequate controls and practices selection, implementation, performancemeasurement, monitoring or auditing.	Conway. B.A., 2010; Juhani. A. et al., 2013.
Inadequate information system auditingin the organization.	Abawajy, J., 2014.; Tim Bedford., 2015.
Weak identifying processing and preserving digital evidence in a mannerthat is legally acceptable.	Bill. G. et al., 2016;Applegate., 2009.
Insufficient enforcement of law.	Brill. A. et al., 2013; Todd. F., 2016.

However, another key element that contributes to SoE attack risks is management defeats in organizations. Management defeats refer to the weaknesses of a safeguard in an asset that organizations do not aware of, are more likely to occur, or are more likely to occur frequently. There are seven (7) common SoE attack risks of management defeats in organizations identified from the previous literature review. Management defeats in organizations include disgruntle of service provider staff, unaddressed service provider responsibility for information security and confidentiality in the contract, staff negligence of service providers such as programmers, technical architecture, testers and, managers; service provider exploitation control weakness in the processes and disgruntled or untrained or ignorant employees who make genuine if human errors. Table 2.6 describes the (7) seven SoE attack risks of management defects in organizations identified from the various previous literature reviews used in this study.

Table 2.6: Literature on the risk of managing defeats attacking the SoE in organizations

SoE attacking risks of management defeats inorganization's item	Literature references
Disgruntle of service provider staff.	Nina Godbole 2017; Christopher. H., 2018; Noor. H. et al, 2007.
Unaddressed service provider's responsibility for information security and confidentiality in the contract.	Nina Godbole 2017;Hinson. G., 2013; Jean Boltz., 2015.
Staff negligent of service providersuch as programmer, technical architecture, tester and manager.	Nina Godbole 2017; Gerben. S. et al., 2015.
Service provider exploitation control weakness in the processes.	Hartini. S., 2013; Joseph. F.et al., 2016.
Disgruntled or untrained or ignorant employees who makegenuine mistake.	Rahul Singh, 2015; Jean Boltz., 2015; Nik. Z. et al., 2010.
Lack of suitable management andcontrol over the user password.	Rahul Singh., 2015; Hinson G, 2013.
Unorganized access control andprivilege on user application account.	Todd. F., 2016; Posey. C.et al., 2015.

However, other key elements that contribute to the risk of an SoE attack are unexpected changes in management. Unexpected change in management refers to rapid change in organizations in which employees sometimes feel difficult to adopt and this type of activity comes from a service provider. There are nine (9) common SoE attack risks of unexpected changes in management identified from the literature. Unexpected changes in management, such as loss of confidentiality of classification information, lack of business continuity plan management and frequent changes in business policies, insufficient attention has been given to the human factors of SoE attacks in design implementation, and a lack of responsibility for digital evidence owners. Table 2.7 describes the (7) seven SoE attack risks of unexpected changes in management identified from various previous literature reviews used for this study.

Table 2.7: Literature on the risk of unexpected change in management resulting from SoE attacks

SoE attacking risks of unexpected change in the management's item	Literature references
Loss of confidentiality of classification information.	Rahul Singh, 2015; Nik. Z. et al., 2016; Noor. H. et al., 2010.
Lack of business continuity plan management.	Rahul Singh, 2015; Jean Boltz., 2015.
Frequently change in business policies.	Noor. H. et at., 2010.
Insufficient attention to human factorsof SoE attacks in design implementation.	Nina Godbole., 2017; Jean Boltz., 2015; Noor. H. et al, 2010.
Lack of information assets owners responsibility.	Jean Boltz., 2015; Nik. Z. et al, 2018.
Unethical competitors (trade secrets, customer list etc).	Nina Godbole, 2017; Noor. H., et al, 2007; Hinson G, 2012.
Severely affect the business survivability of organization.	Todd. F., 2016; Hinson G, 2016; Nik. Z. et al., 2019.
Directly exploit control weakness in the systems.	Nina Godbole, 2017; Nik. Z. et al., 2010; Nina Godbole., 2017.
Lack of security training and awareness regarding SoE attacks	Rahul Singh, 2015; Jean Boltz., 2015; Nina Godbole., 2017.

Thus far, another key element that contributes to SoE attack risks is digital evidence. Digital evidence refers to electronic evidence. The main target of SoE attackers is to collect data or information, which is organizational digital evidence and server data or organizational computer data. Therefore, organizational digital evidence is an asset, and a loss of assets means that an organization is at risk. There have been six (6) Common SoE attack risk of digital evidence identified from the previous literature review. Digital evidence such as - legal activity and documentation, digital documentation of policy and procedures, organization policy of employee online information, updates, and digital evidence must be preserved and held up according to the court of Evidence Act. Table 2.8 describes the (6) six SoE attack risks of digital evidence identified from the various previous literature reviews used in this study.

Table 2.8: Literature on the risk of managing defeats attacking the SoE in organizations

SoE attacking risks of digital evidence item	Literature references
Legal activity and documentation.	Sundresan Perumal, 2009; Rahul Singh, 2015; Hinson G, 2012; Nik. Z.et al., 2016; Suci et al., 2017.
Digital documentation of policy andprocedure.	Sundresan Perumal, 2009; Suci etal., 2017;
Organization policy of employee onlineinformation update.	Siti Rahayu et al., 2008; Suci et al., 2017.
Digital Evidence must be preserved and hold up according in court Evidence Act.	Siti Rahayu et a l.,2008; Jean Bolt z., 2015; Suci et al., 2017.
Organizational perception of Evidence Act.	Siti Rahayu et al., 2008; Jean Boltz., 2015; Suci et al., 2017.
Digital Evidence perception for risk Management importance for SoE attacking risk control.	Mustaruddin et al., 2010; Jean Boltz., 2015; Suci et al., 2017.

Around the globe, SoE attacks such as phishing, spam, intrusion, Trojan horse malware, sabotage of disgruntled employees and stealing data for monetary gains are not uncommon. A survey of 2506 organizations conducted by the Federal Bureau of Investigation (FBI) revealed that in the U.S.A. alone, social engineering attacks and similar crimes cost U.S. businesses a staggering U.S. 57.2 billion a year. This trend is similar in Malaysia, where the number of cases reported to their respective International Computer Emergency Response Teams (ICERT) is increasing.

Moreover, the information security incidents reported to the China in CERT in 2017 were SoE attacks, such as phishing, trojan horse malware, SMS spoofing attack vectors, wireless access point attack, vectors, and third-party modules, which represented 11668, 2293, 1329, 1197 and 1157, respectively.

Various organizations should be able to manage and control the aggressive growth of these risk incidents related to SoE attacks to minimize the losses of digital evidence. Therefore, highlighting the risk of SoE attacks in various types of organizations is necessary to evaluate andmanage them effectively. However, there is still a significant gap in the research investigating SoEattack risks in organizations.

As mentioned earlier, the organization consists of five main phases. The first phase is the analysis of decisions inside the organization. This step concerns the decision of whether to consider the possibility of an SoE attacking risk. Confidentiality, integrity and availability are the three key concepts of information security requirements that prevent SoE attacks. Therefore, SoE attack risk studies are the domain of study in the area of information security. Therefore, confidentiality, integrity and availability are required to ensure security.

The second phase involves the selection of the service provider. It is important to select the service provider who may emphasize SoE attack risk management and who can provide a secure environment for their clients. Hence, the confidentiality, integrity and availability of risks to the organization's digital evidence sufficiently managed the prevention technique of SoE attacks. Additionally, the organization should monitor the service provider's activities to have better control of SoE attack risks and maintain the security of digital evidence in the organization.

Consideration of SoE attack risks comprises five phases of organizational activities, which is relevant because the validation of these activities has been confirmed by previous studies. From the extensive literature review, key principles of information security (CIA) were used to categorize the nature of SoE attack risk, which are classified as digital evidence confidentiality of SoE attack risks, and digital evidence integrity of SoE attack risks and digital evidence availability of SoE attack risks. Table 2.9 describes several SoE attack risks and their nature.

Table 2.9: SoE attack risks based on the confidentiality, integrity and availability (CIA) concept.

SoE attacking risks	**Nature of risks**
Organizational digital evidence leakage.	Confidentiality
Extraction of loss of valuable or private information (BusinessesRecords and client's profiles).	Confidentiality

SoE attacking risks	Nature of risks
Introduction of unauthorized or malicious software through the widespread unauthorized and uncontrolled use of portable devices and transportable computer media.	Confidentiality
Severely affect the business survivability of organization due to lackof BCM and DRP	Availability, Integrity
Poor SoE attack studies, risk assessment practice or excessive orotherwise inadequate controls and practices selection.	Availability, Integrity
Unauthorized exploitation of intellectual property (IP) including plagiarism.	Confidentiality
Disruption of organizational routines and processes with consequentinterruption to trading capabilities, loss of income.	Availability, Integrity
Direct information loss through information theft and fraud (devaluation of organizational image).	Confidentiality, Availability
Loss of confidence in IT, seeding doubts and holding back validcommercial or noncommercial exploitation of IT.	Availability, Integrity
Loss of competitive advantage.	Confidentiality, Integrity

The International Organization of Standardization (ISO) defines information confidentiality as ensuring that information is accessible only to those authorized to access. The confidentiality of information, also called the 'confidentiality bubble,' restricts information flow, with both positive and negative consequences. In the case of SoE attacks, risks such as selected threats or vulnerabilities may contribute to digital evidence confidentiality risks. For example, in social engineering attacks, information leakage is one of the risks likely to materialize during organizational information security, and this incident is caused by SoE attacks.

In information security, integrity means that data or information cannot be modified without authorization. Information integrity issues or incidents usually occur when unauthorized users delete or modify important data files, when a trojan horse malware infects a computer, when unauthorized users vandalize a website, or when someone is able to cast a very large number of votes in an online poll. The integrity of data or information in an organization requires serious monitoring, as the parties involved in the organization may misuse their authorization and access, hence contributing to SoE attacks and increasing risk.

For an information system to serve its purpose, digital evidence must be immediately available when needed. This means that the computing system or mobile device used to store and process digital evidence, the security control used to protect it, and the communication channels used to access it must function at optimum levels. High -availability systems aim to maintain function at all times, preventing service disruptions due to power outages, hardware failures and system upgrades. Information availability risks during an ongoing monitoring process could be the most critical risks to handle since they form part of the service provider. SoE attack risks may contribute to the failure of normal organizational work thus, identifying such risks is vital.

Table 2.10: Shows common SoE attack risks during organizational activities.

Phases in the organization	SoE attacking risks	References
Analysis of decision in the organization.	Information leakage, poor SoE attacking risks study.	Algarni, et al., 2017; Amanda. A. et al., 2003; Georg. D., 2014.
Selection of service provider.	Unauthorized exploitation of intellectual property rights (IPR).	Heidi. W. et al., 2016; Marian, C. et al., 2017; Todd. F., 2016); Veiga. A. etal., 2009.
Contract Management.	digital evidence leakage.	Applegate, et al., (2009); Juhani. A. et al., 2013; Hinson. G., 2011.
On-Going Monitoring.	Environmental Disaster, digital evidence leakage.	Heidi. W. et al., 2014; Hawkins. S. et al., 2000; Bill. G. et al., 2016.

2.4. Fundamental Risk Management Concepts

Risk and management have been studied in a variety of fields, such as insurance, economics, management, medicine, and operation research and engineering. Each field addresses risk in a fashion relevant to its object of analysis and adopts a particular perspective. Hence, the literature reveals several conceptualizations of risk and risk management applications. These multiple perspectives, which are relevant to the study of risk in organizations, are summarized in Table 2.11.

Table 2.11: Summarization of the organizations

Risk Perspective	Description	Reference
Risk as an undesirable event	Risks are the multiple undesirable events that may occur in organizations This perspective is widely used in many fields of studies.	Ayesha. M. et al., 2013); Lund. S. et al., 2015.
Risk as a probabilityfunction	Insurance adopts this perspective and uses mortality tables to estimate probabilities. In this context, a "good risk" will be a person with a low probability of during within a given period (and hence, for the insurance company, a low probability of havingto pay a compensation) and a "bad risk" would be a person with a high probability of dying within the period.	Duff.A., 2007; Ana. F. et al., 2016.
Risk as variance	Finance adopts a different perspective of risk, where risk is equated to the variance of the distribution of outcomes. The extent of the variability in results (whether positive or negative) is the measure of risk. Riskmanagement means arbitrating between risk and returns.	Aubert. et al., 2015;Bill. G. et al,.2016.
Risk as expected loss	Car insurance adopt a perspective of risk as expected loss, they define risk as the product of two function: a loss function and a probability function.	Christopher. H., 2013.

Basically, risk management is an activity directed toward assessing, mitigating and monitoring risks. Risk management helps to answer questions such as whether passing on the new database upgrade will increase changes in being hacked. The need to implement a secure email system, and whether to purchase the latest intrusion-detection technology will reduce the likelihood that web servers will be successfully attacked. Furthermore, risk management helps prioritize issues. Prioritization helps determine the more critical issues to resolve and the subsequent allocation of available resources. This generates productivity gains, especially for organizations that have limited resources and are unable to address all risk areas simultaneously.

2.5. Risk Management for the Prevention Technique of SoE Attacks

Since the early days of information security risk studies in the late 1990s, there has been explosive growth in the development of frameworks, methodologies, management studies and standards to safeguard digital evidence. Although SoE attacking risks is the domain of study in information security risk. Therefore, managing risk is the basic precept for managing SoE attack risks. Securing management should be part of the agency's overall risk management. These findings point to the need for appropriate risk management for the prevention of SoE attacks and for the use of this approach to cater to specific issues in organizations. Although several information security risk management approaches have been developed that focus on specific areas (such as OCTAVE, CORAS, ISRAM and COBIT), limited research has been conducted on managing the risks of preventing SoE attacks in organizations. There is a lack of evidence on the specific strategies used for risk management involving the prevention technique of SoE attacks in organizations and which strategies are most important, as conditioned by organizational and economic restraints. The ISC2 common body of knowledge (CBK) is an organization and collection of relevant information security professionals, such as security policy, organizational security, personal security, access control, compliance, business continuity, system development and maintenance, communication and operations management, asset classification and control and physical environmental security, personal security, access control, compliance, business continuity, system development and maintenance, communication and operation management, asset classification and control and physical environment security. The organization ISC2 also highlights security management as another significant domain relevant to the information security body of knowledge, in dealing with prevention techniques for SoE attack issues. The domain emphasizes the importance of a comprehensive security plan that includes security policies and procedures for protecting data and how they are administered.

The management of prevention techniques for SoE attacks in organizations must approach maintaining the confidentiality, availability, integrity, nonrepudiation, accountability, authenticity and reliability of organizational systems. Commonly, information might be improperly disclosed because its confidentiality could be exposed or modified in an inappropriate way because its integrity could be jeopardized and destroyed or lost because its availability could be threatened. Risk management and analysis have become key components of preventing SoE attacks. Risk management and analysis for security management is an important approach for determining which security controls are appropriate and cost effective for specific environments and organizations.

In sum, risk management for the prevention of SoE attacks is a concept in which a systematic approach is used to control SoE attack risk and develop an appropriate protection strategy as a major component of protecting digital evidence.

2.6. Risk Management Methodologies and Approaches for the Prevention Technique of SoEAttacks

At present, numerous comprehensive prevention techniques for SoE attack risk guides integrating various approaches have been developed to encourage best practices of risk management for the prevention of SoE attacks and to ensure that digital evidence remains secure. The available risk management practices for preventing SoE attacks, methodologies and analysis approaches are either qualitative or quantitative in nature. These methodologies have the common goal of estimating overall risk. The risk management methodology used was OCTAVE provided a qualitative information security risk analysis for the information and communication technology. Moreover, quantitative methodologies are available through the Information Security Risk Analysis Method (ISRAM). Information System Analysis based on a Business Model and Cost-Of -Risk Analysis (CORA).

Another initiative is to strengthen ICT security management. The guideline emphasizes information security risk assessment steps to identify and evaluate information security risks for self – -development or in -house organization implementation. These guidelines have also been used to assess information security risk levels in government agencies through organizations' high-level risk assessments. Even though the guidelines are considered comprehensive, they concern more in – -house development within the organization. However, this approach is still insufficient because it does not include proper consideration of SoE attack risk issues.

Furthermore, an appropriate framework for preventing SoE attacks on risk management is needed. Currently, addressing specific SoE attack risks is considered crucial. Thus, different risk factors could arise, and the proposed framework would differ from those preceding it. Other related risk assessment approaches and tools used to manage information security risks include historical analysis, event tree analysis, failure mode and effect analysis, probabilistic risk assessment, human error analysis and HAZOP (hazard and operability). Table 2.12 describes various information security risk management concepts, methodologies and approaches.

Table 2.12: Information Security Risk Management Concepts, Methodologies and Approaches

Related Risk Management Methodology and Approach	Description	References
OCTAVE	Approach concentrates on assets, threats andvulnerabilities.	Algarni, A. et al., 2017.
CORAS	Integration of risk management and systems development process as one of the pillars to focus on lies on the tight integration of viewpoint oriented UML – like modeling in risk management process.	Peltier. T., 2012.
Information Security Risk Analysis Methodology (ISRAM)	Security based model applying a quantitativeapproach to risk analysis that allows for participation of the management and staff of the organization but does not use techniques such as single occurrence losses (SOL) or annual loss expectancy (ALE).	Mohamed, N. et al., 2013.
Cost-of-Risk Analysis (CORA)	Risk Model uses data collection on threat function and assets and vulnerabilities of the function and assets to the threats to calculate the consequences, which are the loses due to the occurrences of the threats.	Louis. A., 2010.
Event Tree Analysis	Translation of the failure behavior of a physical system into a visual diagram and logic model. Event trees, attack trees and fault trees.	Clif Ericson, 2016.
Historical Analysis	Examines frequency of past incidents to determine the probability of recurrence.	Clif Ericson. 2016.
Human error analysis	Studies the possible impact of human error andintervention.	Marian, C. etal., 2017.

Related Risk Management Methodology and Approach	Description	References
Probabilistic Risk Assessment	Investigates the probability that a combinationof events will lead to a particular condition (Quantitative Risk Analysis, originated from across space program, 1960s)	Nik. Z.et al., 2018; Tim Bed ford., 2016.
Failure Model and effect analysis	Examines each potential failure condition in the system to determine the severity of the impact.	Sumner, M., 2011; Peltier, T., 2016.
HAZOP (Hazardand operability)	Examines process and engineering intentions to access the potential hazards (Risk) that canarise from deviation in design specifications.	Nik. Z. et al., 2018.
Information System (IS) analysis based on a business model.	Defines assets value, based the analysis on itsreplacement cost and measures the tangible assets value from the viewpoint of operational continuity.	Suit & Han., 2008.
Malaysian CyberSecurity	Malaysian organization Risk Assessment guideline and methodologies focuses on ICTsecurity, vulnerabilities, threats and safeguards for information assets in the organization.	Malaysian Cyber Security., 2019.
HiLRA	Malaysian Public Sector Information SecurityHigh level Risk Assessment	National Library of Malaysia., 2019.

2.7. Information security framework for the prevention technique of SoE attacks, Standardsand Guidelines

A review of several related information security standards and guidelines available in the industry provides ideas on how to develop a dedicated information security risk management framework for the prevention technique of SoE attacks, for organizations. For example, the standards and guidelines for risk management and analysis for security management extensively described in the ISO/IEC 27000 Series and ISO/IEC 27005 provide insight into information security risk management. It supports the general concepts specified in ISO/IEC 27001 and is designed to assist the satisfactory implementing information security based on a risk management approach. Knowledge of the concepts, models, processes and terminologies described in ISO/IEC 27001 and ISO/IEC 27002, is important for obtaining a better understanding of ISO/IEC 27005. The ISO/IEC 27005 is applicable to all types of organizations (e.g. Commercial enterprise, government agencies, and nonprofit organizations), which intend to manage risks that could compromise the organization's information security. Fundamentally, the concepts provided in the standards emphasize the value of a risk management approach for preventing SoE attacks.

Researchers have claimed that information security is an organization's approach to maintaining the confidentiality, availability, accountability, integrity, nonrepudiation, accountability, authenticity and reliability of its IT/ICT system Moreover, identifying and analyzing risk factors for SoE attacks are key components of a security management plan for preventing SoE attacks. Risk management of SoE attacks relies on an information security risk management strategy to ensure that digital evidence is secure. The details of these approaches are explicitly defined in the Management Program and plan for the prevention technique of SoE attacks. Table 2.13 briefly describes the related framework, standards and guidelines used as sources of reference in conducting this work.

Table 2.13: Information Security Management Standards and Guidelines.

Information Security Management Standards or Guidelines	Description	References
ISO 27001 (Global Standard)	Information Security as a combination of people, process and technology.	Mohamed. G. et al., 2016.
ISO/IEC 27007 (Global Standard)	Overview and vocabulary: Information Technology Secure technique – Informationsecurity management Systems.	Neeta. S. et al., 2016; Malaysian Cyber Security, 2019; Parker. D., 2017.

Information Security Management Standards or Guidelines	Description	References
ISO/IEC 13335-1 GMITS (Global Standard)	Part1: Concepts and models for information and communication technologysecurity management (Descriptions of the major security elements and their relationships that are involved in ICT security management) Current revised title is BS ISO/IEC 13335-1	MAMPU., 2018.
ISO/IEC 13335-2 GMITS (Global Standard)	Part 2: Information Security Risk Management (Standards originally from Switzerland. Currently widely user Current revised title is ISO/IEC 27005	Malaysian Cyber Security,2018; Christopher.H., 2018.
ISO/IEC 13335-3 GMITS (Global Standard)	Guidelines of the Management of IT Security Part 3: Techniques for the management of IT Security.	Malaysian Cyber Security., 2018; Christopher. H., 2018.
ISO/IEC 13335-4 GMITS (Global Standard)	Guidelines for the management of IT Security Part 4: Selection of safeguards. Current revised title is ISO/IEC 13335-4	MAMPU, 2018; Christopher.H., 2015.
ISO/IEC 13335-5 GMITS (Global Standards)	Guidelines for the management of IT Security Part 5: Management Guideline on Network Security. Currently revised title is ISO/IEC TR 13335-5	Malaysian Cyber Security, 2018; Cooke. M. et al., 2017.
ISO-IEC 14516 (Global Standard)	Guidelines for the management of Trusted Third Parties Services. Current revised titleis ISO/IEC TR 14516	Eloff, M. etal., 2014.
BS 7799 (ISO IEC 17799:2000)- Organization/ Nation	Information technology security technique.Code of practices for Information Security Management (Origin British Standard BS 7799) Current revised title is ISO/IEC 17799:2000 Malaysia Standards MS ISO 17799	Appin Security Group., 2017.
Malaysian Cyber Security	Malaysian organization Management of Information and communication technologySecurity Guideline and methodologies.	Malaysian Cyber Security, 2018

Common digital evidence	Digital evidence characteristics	Common digital evidence
ISO/IEC 15947 (Domain Specific	IT intrusion detection framework (computertechnology, Data Security, Data storage protection, safety measures, Data processing, Information exchange, Data transmission, Risk management Currentrevised title is ISO/IEC TR 15947	Appin Security Group., 2017.
ISO/TR 13569 (Domain Specific)	Information technology security techniques. Information security programmed for financial service industry. Policies, organizations and the structural, legal andregulation components. Selection and implementation of security controls. Elements required to manage informationsecurity risk. Currently revised title is ISO/TR 13569	Malaysian Cyber Security, 2018; Ana. F. et al., 2016.
IETF RFC 2196 (Domain Specific	Site/web security Handbook Guide to developing computer security policies andprocedures for sites that have systems on the internet. Provide practical guidance toadministrators trying to secure them information and services. Web security Risk Assessment or Analysis.	Jean Boltz., 2016.

Through robust understanding of the current standards and guidelines, this research attempts to establish contexts and findings that are globally and nationally acceptable. Social engineering is the context of the area of information security. The purpose of SoE attacks is to obtain confidential digital evidence from the system. However, the concept of risk management for preventing SoE attacks relies on a systematic approach in which information security risks are assessed for SoE attacks, so that appropriate protection strategies can be developed to form the foundation of an effective information security program. Fundamentally, this principle involves overlapping steps applied at every phase of risk management for the prevention of SoE attacks in the organization. Each step has key elements for developing its objectives at each phase. Risk identification is the primary step in risk management. This involves identifying specific elements of the three risk components, such as digital evidence, threats and vulnerabilities.

However, the specific elements of unexpected change in management and management defeats of SoE attack risks are also connected with organizational digital evidence. The first step in determining the appropriate level of security involves identifying an organization's digital evidence and determining its value. This conceptual framework adopts relevant qualitative and quantitative digital evidence valuation methods. Second, risk analysis must be conducted in various ways. Effective risk analysis brings combines all the elements of risk management (identification, analysis, response and monitoring) and is critical in developing an effective risk management strategy. This is followed by risk response, as a properly conducted risk analysis enables the selection of appropriate safeguards and countermeasures. A safeguard controls or reduces the risks associated with specific SoE attack risks of vulnerabilities without safeguarding. The risk of threats caused by SoE attack will turn into a risk of attack; thus, increasing risks and threats and vulnerability will turn to the risk of attack by management defeats in organizations, the risk of unexpected change and the risk of attack by SoE on digital evidence.

Table 2.14: Highlights the basic concepts of risk management for preventing SoE attacks.

Risk Management approach for the prevention technique of SoE attacks	Description	References
Risk identification	A process of identifying the risk to the system's security.	Rahul Singh., 2015; NinaGodbole., 2017.
Risk Analysis	A process of determiningthe probability of occurrences, the resultingimpact and additional safeguards that would mitigate impact.	Rahul Singh., 2015 Nik. Z. et al., 2018; Peltier,T., 2016
Risk Response	Countermeasure that reduce risks associated with specific threats (risks reduction, assignment and transference, avoidance or acceptance).	Nina Godbole., 2017;Georg. D., 2014; JeanBoltz., 2015.

Risk Management approach for the prevention technique of SoE attacks	Description	References
Risk Monitoring	Maintenance of records of incidents, identification new risks and determining if any of the known risks have changed, control andcountermeasure effectiveness, compliance with standards and regulations, providing vulnerabilities and incidentalters, maintaining the risk management plan.	Nina Godbole., 2017; Jean Boltz., 2015.

Identification of risks involves the SoE attack risk of digital evidence valuation, the SoE attack risk of threat analysis and the SoE attack risk of vulnerability assessment. The basic elements required to determine the value of an element required to determine the value of an SoE attack risk of digital evidence are the initial and organizational values. Digital evidence valuation facilities analyze and support management decisions regarding the selection of appropriate safeguards. Identification of SoE attack risks is critical in organizations.

2.8. Expert Judgment Method: Definition of elicitations objectives

One of the key stages in the expert elicitation process is the definition of the problem or issue to be judged. For the purpose of the confirmatory study, the objectives to be achieved were defined as follows:

To collect, combine, and synthesize expert opinions regarding the acceptability of the proposed framework in general organization practices.

To collect, combine and synthesize expert opinions regarding the applicability of the proposed framework in managing SoE attack risk for the organization.

A unique evaluation form was then created to enable the experts to assess the framework and meet the stated objectives. To increase the reliability of the confirmatory study, the expert judgment method was adopted, thus making the identification of appropriate knowledgeable experts to validate the framework components, mandatory. The main criterion for selection was that these personnel have responsibilities and experience in dealing with the organization and SoE attack risk management practices and were acknowledged experts in the related fields. While there has been some positive correlation between years of experience and educational background, there is no evidence to support the universal application of this standard.

Despite the number of years of experience, educational background, cognitive skills, and criteria to be integrated together in the selection process, none of the criteria are considered disqualifiers of expertise, as expertise is an integrated summation of the characteristics (criteria) described. For the purpose of this study, three (3) trials were selected to verify and validate the framework components.

Table 2.15: Characteristics of the experts involved in the confirmatory study

Expert Characteristics	**Expert Characteristics Appropriate to validate and verity the frameworkapplicability and acceptability**
Domain Knowledge: • Years of experience • Education Background • Designation Level	21 years of experience Information Security Professional Certification (CISSP), Master Degree, Chief Information Security Consultant, senior Manager, Certified Professional orspecialist
Cognitive Skills • Ability to differentiate usefulness of data	Knowledge and technical skill about SoE attacking risk and risk management.
Decision Strategies	Expert possess decision making andconsulting roles
Expert-Task Congruence • Appropriate expertise fordiscipline specific task	Similar interests in research subject(SARM) for the organization.

However, the risk management practices for preventing SoE attacks, as suggested and described by other researchers. The SoE is the domain of study in information security. Therefore, it is necessary to review the previous literature to understand information security risk management. However, the gap in the literature is attributed to the fact that most of the researchers who address SoE attack risks are isolated, and only a small number of researchers have produced a structured approach and step-by-step guidelines to manage the risk of SoE attacks in organizations. Crucially, this activity identified various information security approaches where SoE is included and practices recommended by other researchers include OCTAVE, CORAS, information security risk analysis methodology (ISRAM), information system analysis based on a business model, cost-of-risk analysis (CORA), Malaysian Cybersecurity and HiLRA. However, an appropriate design for the prevention technique of the SoE attack framework used in organizations is still unavailable. Less empirical evidence has concentrated on service providers' management practices, which can contribute to developing better risk management approaches for preventing SoE attacks in organizations.

In addition to the risk management practices for SoE attacks, the literature has identified digital evidence involved in such organizations. However, studies on the security requirement levels for these digital evidence sets still pose several questions. The classification of digital evidence security requirements in each organizational activity still needs to be determined clearly based on the core principles for the prevention technique of SoE attacks. Here, information security experts and security professionals would then, be better able to plan appropriate strategies to protect organizational digital evidence from security risks in each phase of organizational activities. Subsequently, risk management practices for preventing SoE attacks and controlling related digital evidence involved in organizations could be implemented effectively, hence minimizing the negative impact of the risk of SoE in the organization. The literature has also suggested various SoE attack risks in organizations. However, whether more than SoE attack risks would occur in organizations still remains to be determined. Therefore, further research should be conducted to determine this phenomenon. Hence, in this research, ten (10) SoE attack risks of threats and twelve (12) SoE attack risks of vulnerabilities, seven (7) SoE attack risks of management defects in the organization, nine (9) SoE attack risks of unexpected changes in management, and six (6) SoE attack risks of digital evidence from the previous literature and scholarly article were used as SoE attack risks in the organization.

In sum, a review of the literature highlights the scarcity of research on risk management for preventing SoE attacks in organizations. The aim of the study thus, is also to contribute to the literature, specifically, to the work on providing guidelines for managing risks in organizations. The focus of the literature that has helped to construct the framework has been the conceptual theories of SoE attack risks, the general concept of digital evidence, risk management fundamentals and information risks, and concepts and guidelines. The inclusion of these theories enhances understanding and strengthens the proposed framework, which is also presented in a structured form to facilitate understanding and application. The related literature and issues highlighted in this chapter point to the need for research on current practices in risk management for the prevention of SoE attacks in organizations.

Chapter Three

Framework Methodology: Processing Data and Threat Landscapes

3.1. Overview of framework methodology

The methodology refers to the manner in which researchers conduct the work. Several methods (such as survey, and experimental methods) are deployed around the world to create newknowledge in specific fields. The three generic research methods are qualitative, quantitative andhybrid or mixed. Qualitative research refers to the what, why, When and how the phenomenon works, while qualitative research refers to how researchers quantify the research subject. Qualitative methods rely on the meaning and definition, concepts, context, descriptions and environmental setting of the study, while, quantitative research relies on measurement and statistics. However, both approaches focus on the importance of objectivity, observation and data collection, although qualitative research by its nature is more dependent on the researcher's subjective interpretation. Qualitative research provides rich descriptions of the phenomenon of study, which requires individuals to see, touch and experiment with activities in the natural environment. However, quantitative research requires sorting, counting and analyzing empirical data using appropriate statistical tools to produce results. In brief, quantitative research reports thestatistical results of the analysis of the study. While there has been great debate on the virtues of each research approach, both approaches are highly respected and can complement each other. When the use of both approaches could lead to the creation of new empirical evidence and knowledge from multiple perspectives. The simultaneous use of quantitative and qualitative methods is referred to as mixed or hybrid. In recent years, researchers from various fields have begun to apply mixed methods techniques to expand the scope of and gain deeper insights from their studies. Crucially, as a methodology, the mixed methods technique augments quantitative studies through qualitative research. This method also validates the concepts, the exploratory studyand the development of the framework. Moreover, expert judgment is used to confirm the proposed framework.

The key objective of the mixed methodology was to explore supporting evidence for thedevelopment of a framework for the management of risk regarding the prevention technique of SoE attacks in organizations. The study approach involved five phases theoretical, empirical, exploratory, framework development and confirmatory. In each phase, the activities involved in the research process were described. This chapter explains each of the phases and activities involved in this mixed methods approach.

Table 3.1: Study activities and objectives.

	Objective 1	**Objective 2**	**Objective 3**	**Objective 4**
Research Objectives	To identify various SoE attacking risks.	To analyze SoE attacking risks in various organization such as healthcare, banking , education and government agencies.	To integrate SoE attacking risks with SoE attacking risk management for developing of information security framework for the prevention technique of SoE attacks.	To develop information security framework for the prevention technique of SoE attacks through expert judgment.

	Theoretical Study	**Empirical Study**	**Exploratory Study**	**Framework Development**	**Confirmatory Study**
	Information gathering	Identify Research Construct and attributes	Identify the risk management practice for the prevention technique of SoE attacks in the organizations	Compile and consolidate empirical and exploratory findings.	Verify the proposed framework through expert judgment.

	Theoretical Study	**Empirical Study**	**Exploratory Study**	**Framework Development**	**Confirmatory Study**
Research activity	Identify related theoretical aspect and concept of the study.	Conduct statistical analysis	Semi structured way was used.	Identify components of proposed framework.	Conclude confirmatory findings.
	Design Data collection tools.	Conclude empirical findings.	To access and analyze organizational risk management	Develop proposed framework.	
			To integrate SoE attacking risks with risk management practices for develop information security framework		
			Conclude exploratory findings.		

The study methodology involved data collection and data analysis methods and activities. A detailed explanation of each method and technique is included in the next section. As the study deployed quantitative and qualitative methods, the quantitative approach was first used to measure and describe connections and variables on a specific scale to enable the testing of specific hypotheses. Subsequently, a qualitative approach, which concerns human phenomena and seeks to uncover the meaning that people attach to specific experiences, was adopted. While a quantitative research methodology was initially used, confirmatory research utilizing qualitative methods was later required to further validate the results of the quantitative study.

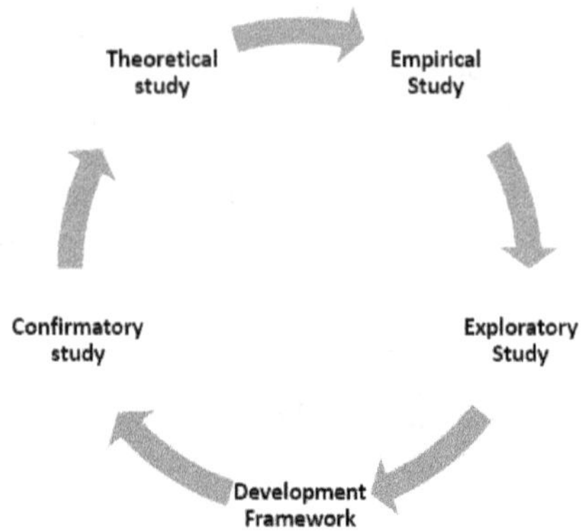

Figure 3.1: Provides an overview of the methodology adopted for the study.

Theoretical Study:

1. Literature review of the theoretical background and fundamental concepts.
2. Questionnaire design and plot study.

Empirical Study:

1. The questionnaire was distributed to 384 respondents from various organizations, such asbanking sectors, healthcare centers, education sectors and government agencies.
2. Empirical analysis (SoE attack risks, SoE attack risk management practices).

Explore further empirical results:

1. Hypothesis testing and other relevant statistical testing.
2. Analysis (Results and Findings)

Exploratory Study:

1. A semi-structured approach was used to reveal relevant information. To identify the SoE attack risk management practices in the organization.

Framework development

1. Reanalyze the results from previous findings (empirical and exploratory)
2. Identify the framework's components.
3. A critical review of existing theories, models, frameworks and related documents is still needed.
4. Draft framework for confirmatory study.

Confirmatory Study through Expert Judgment:

1. Framework validation by experts in related fields.
2. Verify the reliability and acceptability of the framework.

3.2. Theoretical study

A theoretical study defines the fundamental theories and key concepts of the framework as well as the variables and components involved in the study. This phase involved the gathering of information related to the research areas organizations such as banking sectors, education sectors, and healthcare sectors; and government agencies. SoE attack risks and risk management practices for preventing SoE attacks in organizations. This theoretical study focuses on the relevant literature to determine the framework and concept of the research as well as related theories supporting the related research activities. The main aims of this theoretical study are to highlight the knowledge gap in the literature to introduce the problem statement, objectives, and significance of the study; and to conceptualize the framework prior to conducting the activity. Subsequent to synthesizing the theoretical foundations and key concepts, data collection tools for the pilot study were also developed. The exploration of the inputs, approaches and results of the conceptual and theoretical study phases are illustrated in Table 3.2.

Table 3.2: Theoretical Study Phase: Study Approach.

Input	Research Approach (process)	Results(output)
Article, Books, Journals, Conference Proceeding, Magazine, News, Online Database Journal, ISO Standard Guidelines, Research Article.	Review related area to study. Access online journal database. Identify issues in the knowledge research areas. Identify knowledge gap of the study. Design questionnaire forpilot study.	Literature review summary. Established area of research. Theoretical foundation and key concept of study. Pilot questionnaire.

Input	**Research Approach (process)**	**Results(output)**
Pilot questionnaire.	Validate pilot questionnairethrough Expert –Judgment approach. Reliability Test.	Refined questionnaire (validated)

This research begins with an extensive literature review of relevant articles, theories and concepts from three interrelated knowledge sources. A review of published documents was performed to better identify the knowledge gap. The conceptual study focused on three knowledge areas, organizational activity, social engineering attack risks and risk management practices, for the prevention of SoE attacks. Other related concepts and theories were also reviewed as supplementary support for the theoretical study. Throughout the review, the best practices that led to success in risk management for the prevention technique of SoE attacks in the organization were identified. These identified practices proved the key considerations for developing the research framework for the prevention technique of SoE attacks in organizations, which is the major contribution of the study. Theories and concepts are pivotal in formulating the theoretical framework of the study. A theory makes generalizations about observations and consists of an interrelated. A coherent set of ideas and models, while a concept is an image of symbolic representations of an abstract idea. Concepts have been defined as complex mental formulations of experience. The theoretical framework is the theory on which the study is based.

The theoretical framework reflects the position and gives direction to the study. The model used in a previous study. may have been adopted. These modifications are appropriate for the inquiry. In addition to providing the direction of the study, through the theoretical framework, the researcher is able to show the relationships among the different constructs to be investigated. Generally, the theoretical framework was developed to structure and organize several theories and concepts related to the study for further investigation.

3.3. SoE attack risks of threats and vulnerability effects on digital evidence

Beyond the principle of basic security fundamentals, the concept of risk management is the most important and complex part of SoE attacks and risk management in the information security domain. Risk management for preventing SoE attacks is primarily concerned with the risk of SoE attack threats and vulnerabilities that can affect digital evidence. The SoE attack risk of threats refers to any natural or manmade circumstances or events that could have an adverse or undesirable impact on organizational digital evidence. Moreover, this approach exploits the weakness of the system to protect digital evidence. The SoE attack risk of vulnerabilities refers to the presence of weakness in a system to protect digital evidence, which can potentially cause system weakness increase the harm or cost of the system and increase the likelihood of occurrence or frequent occurrence. In the proposed conceptual framework, digital evidence is an asset in the system that has some value for an organization and is therefore protected.

The threats and vulnerabilities of SoE attack risks have a great influence on the organization. This could occur because service providers may not reveal the proper identity of their services that could contribute to the risk of contracting SoE. Digital evidence may be tangible, such as computer data, software and records, or intangible, such as privacy, access, public image and ethics, and may likewise have tangible value (purchase price) or intangible value (competitive advantage). Therefore, the conceptual framework focuses on digital evidence as an asset, including documented (paper or electronic) information or intellectual information that is used to meet the mission or objective of the organization.

As a matter of the principle of basic security fundamentals, the concepts of risk management are the most important and complex part of SoE attacks and risk management in the information security domain. Risk management for the prevention technique of SoE is primarily concerned with the risk of SoE attacking management defects and the risk of SoE attacking unexpected changes in management, influencing the risk of SoE attacking digital evidence. Apart from the risk of the threat and vulnerability, of the SoE attack, two other drivers are the risk of the SoE attack on management defeats in the organization and the risk of the SoE attack.

As a matter of the principle of basic security fundamentals, the concepts of risk management are the most important and complex part of SoE attacks and risk management in the information security domain. Risk management for the prevention technique of SoE is primarily concerned with the risk of SoE attacking management defects and the risk of SoE attacking unexpected changes in management, influencing the risk of SoE attacking digital evidence. Apart from the risk of the threat and vulnerability, of the SoE attack, two other drivers are the risk of the SoE attack on management defeats in the organization and the risk of the SoE attack risk of unexpected change in management in the organization. Management defeats refer to any natural or man -made circumstances or events in which employees in the organization cannot know how to do so or lack the resources or knowledge needed to protect the digital evidence in the organization. The SoE attack risk of unexpected change refers to unawareness among employees or the absence of proper training to protect digital evidence. Hence, losing this digital evidence could potentially have a negative impact on the service provider activities in the organization. The proposed conceptual framework shows the process or system that has some value to an organization and therefore is protected. The SoE attacks the risk of management defeating in an organization, and the risk of unexpected change in management could influence the organization and could contribute to risk incidents of SoE attacks. Digital evidence may be tangible, such as computer data, software and records, or intangible, such as privacy, access, public image and ethics, and may likewise have tangible value (purchase price) or intangible value (competitive advantage). Therefore, the conceptual framework focuses on protecting digital evidence, such as documented (paper or electronic) information or intellectual property, which is used to meet the mission and objective of the work.

The basic security fundamentals, the concepts of the SoE attack risk of threats, the SoE attack risk of vulnerability, the SoE attack risk of management defeats in the organization and the SoE attack risk of unexpected change in management are the most common SoE attack risks in the information security domain and have a great influence on the SoE attack risk of digital evidence. Risk management for the prevention technique of SoE attacks the primary concern of protecting digital evidence as an organizational tool asset. Digital evidence refers to any evidence, stored on a computer server, physical hard drive or mobile device. However, loss of this digital evidence can be a catastrophic incident and potentially impact the organization. Hence, loss of digital evidence is a great risk to the organization. The proposed conceptual framework shows that digital evidence is an asset in the organization, therefore protection from SoE attacks is needed. Whereas the SoE attacks the risk of threats, the SoE attacks the risk of vulnerabilities, and the SoE attacks the risk of management defeats in an organization the SoE attacks the risk of unexpected change in management and has a great influence on the digital evidence in the organization because malicious persons or SoE attackers usually target digital evidence in the organization. Moreover, losing this digital evidence may have a negative impact on the organization. In fact, assets, such as computer data, software and records, may be tangible, or intangible assets, such as privacy, access, public image and ethics, may likewise have tangible value (purchase price) or intangible value (competitive advantage). Therefore, the conceptual framework focuses on protecting digital evidence from SoE attacks and is used to meet the mission or objective of the work.

The risk management plan for preventing SoE attacks is another vital concept on which the study is based. This concept requires practitioners to integrate risk identification of SoE attacks and analysis results to format an appropriate management plan for the prevention technique of SoE attacks to monitor risks. Moreover, rigorous standards and guidelines such as the ISO/IEC 27000 series are used as a reference source for formulate an internationally acceptable management plan for preventing SoE attacks. The plan details the specific actions needed of the information security professional to protect organizational information digital evidence. Furthermore, the plan includes steps on how organizations respond to and monitor risk incidents of SoE attacks caused by threats and vulnerabilities. Information security professionals must also include how the appropriate response measures for management plans for preventing SoE attacks are implemented based on the risk analysis conducted. In essence, the plan will provide detailed strategies on how to minimize the occurrence of SoE attacking incidents and their impact on organizations' business activities.

3.4. Questionnaire Design

Based on the concepts and theoretical foundations, literature review and research questions, however, the questionnaire of the constructs proposed in this study was developed through expert judgment. The constructs and attributes in the questionnaire were also tested using a reliability test.

Figure 3.2: Development of the questionnaire for the purpose of this study.

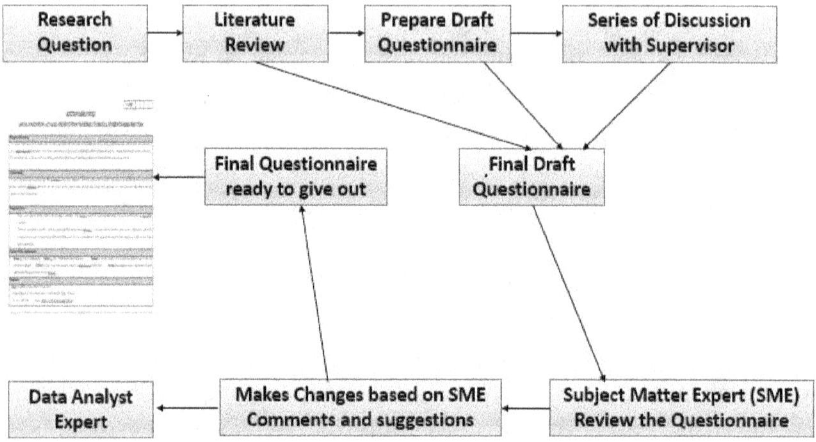

Figure: 3.2: Data collection tool (questionnaire) design flow

Two Subject Matter Experts (SMEs) were appointed to validate the questionnaire constructs, one being an academic expert (PhD) and the other being a manager in the organization (with more than 7 years of experience in the organization). Based on the comments and suggestions of the SMEs, improvements were made to the entire questionnaire, which was further reviewed and verified by the experts before distribution. Figure 3.3 shows the structure and overview of the questionnaire content.

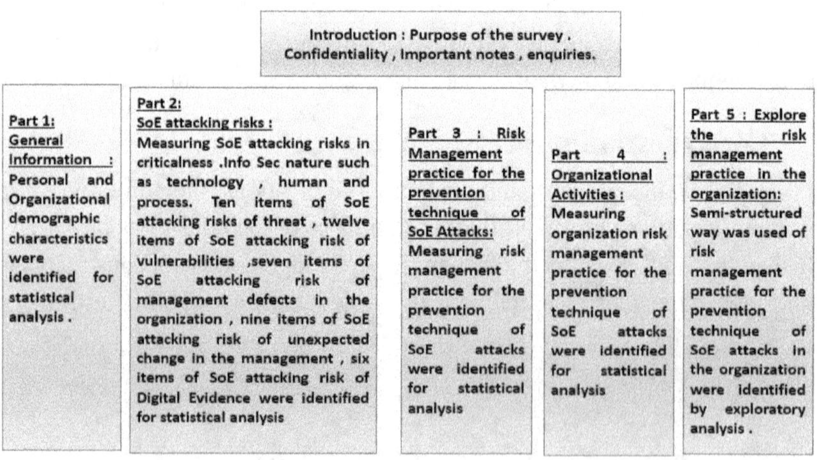

Figure 3.3: Overview structure and content of the questionnaire

A refined questionnaire was distributed to investigate the factors that influence the practice of preventing SoE attack risks and to assess SoE attack risk management practices as well as digital evidence security requirements in the organization.

3.5. Pilot Study Results Summary

A pilot study was conducted to test the validity and reliability of the constructs and attributes of the questionnaire and validate the respondents' understanding of the content of the questionnaires. A total of 89 questionnaires were distributed to various organizational sectors. Of these, 30 were returned, and their data were analyzed. The participants were informed of the objectives of the pilot study which were to assess the quality of the questionnaire, thus highlighting the importance of their feedback and comments. The pilot study analysis results describe the reliability of the constructs and attributes developed in the questionnaire. After receiving feedback, the questionnaire was further refined before its eventual distribution. The demographic profile of the respondents, including their name (optional), organizational name, position, gender, age, personal working experience, level of work and experience with SoE attacks, was examined. The pilot study was performed in various organizations. As stated, 89 questionnaires were distributed, and 30 responses were obtained, indicating that 33% of the responses were for analysis. However, for the banking sector, the percentage of respondents was 36%, for the education sector, the percentage of respondents was 30%; for the healthcare sector, the percentage of respondents was 17% and for the government agency, the percentage of respondents was 17%.

Hence, within these four organizations, the male and female response rates were 54% and 46%, respectively. Considering the respondent ages, 26 to 30, years, 13% of the respondents were aged 31 to 35 years, 23% were aged between 36 and 40 years, 20% were aged between 41 and 50 years, 36% were aged between 46 and 50 years, 5% were aged at 5%, and 3% were aged older than 50 years. When considering personal working experience, it was observed that 36% of the participants had less than 5 years of working experience, 20% had working experience between 6 and 10 years, 36% had working experience between 11 and 15 years 15 to 20 years, 5% had working experience and 3% had working experience greater than 20 years. When considering the participants' level of experience, 14% of the respondents were senior managers, 33% were senior managers, and 53% had other levels of employees.

However, the respondents' experience with SoE attacks was considered. The first question asked about suspicious calls or phone calls. Overall, 24% of them had this type of experience and 76% of them did not have this type of experience. Again, the participants were asked about any unexpected mail received regarding organization information or lottery prizes. It was observed that 20% of the employees had this type of experience, while 80% did not. However, employees were asked whether any unauthorized person would enter the organization without proper identification. Fourteen percent of them said that they had noticed this type of activity, and 86% said they did not have this experience at all. Hence, asked to them if they felt any type of incident, what actually they would do. Among them, 23% responded that they would block the number, 30% said they would cancel the call, 16% said they would delete the mail, 20% said they would contract with a security expert and 11% responded that they would block the mail. The last question asked about the respondent's reactivity, whether he or she had this type of experience and how he or she would feel. A total of 83% responded that they would feel disturbed, and 17% responded nothing about this activity.

The pilot study focused particularly on the most common SoE attack risks, such as the SoE attack risk of threats, the SoE attack risk of vulnerabilities, the SoE attack risk of management defeats in organizations, the SoE attack risk of unexpected changes in management, and the SoE attack risk of digital evidence. There are ten (10) SoE attack risks of threat, twelve (12) SoE attack risks of vulnerabilities, seven (7) SoE attack risk of management defects in the organization, nine (9) SoE attack risk of unexpected change in management and six (6) SoE attack risk of digital evidence items identified from the previous literature review. SoE attack risk drivers or constructors were used in the pilot study to test the reliability of the test. Cronbach's alpha coefficient was used to test the reliability of the pilot survey items. A coefficient value closer to "1" was needed. Cronbach's alpha values for SoE attack risk of threats (0.943), SoE attack risk of vulnerabilities (0.924), SoE attack risk of management defeats in organizations (0.910), SoE attack risk of changes in management (0.920), and SoE attack risk of digital evidence (0.950) were high. Since all the items in Table 3.4 below had a reliability of more than 0.7, the scales for these constructs were considered to exhibit acceptable reliability.

Table 3.3: Reliability test of the risk factors associated with SoE attacks (pilot study)

SoE attacking Risks	Items	Cronbach's Alpha value	N
SoE attacking riskof threats	10	0.943	30
SoE attacking risk of vulnerabilities	12	0.924	30
SoE attacking riskof management defeats in organization	7	0.910	30
SoE attacking riskof unexpected changes in management	9	0.920	30
SoE attacking riskof digital evidence	6	0.950	30

Note: Items – Numbers of variables, N –Total Number of Respondents

The pilot study also focused on risk management practices for the prevention technique of SoE attacks in the organizations. The SoE attack risk of threats and the SoE attack risk of vulnerabilities influence the SoE attack risk of management defeats in organizations, and the SoE attack risk of unexpected changes in management these two constructs influence the SoE attack risk of digital evidence, and digital evidence influences risk management practices. Cronbach's alpha coefficient was used to test the reliability of the pilot survey items. A coefficient value closer to "1" was needed. Table 3.6 The results of the reliability test.

Table 3.4: RMs for preventing SoE attacks in the organizations according to the constructed reliability test.

Risk Management Practices for the Prevention Technique of SoE attacks in the organizations	Items	Cronbach's Alpha value	N
Risk managementpractice for SoE attacks	10	0.943	30

Note: Items – Numbers of variables, N –Total Number of Respondents

The pilot study also focused on organizational activities. For the research data collection, four organizations were selected for data collection. The SoE attack risk of threats and the SoE attack risk of vulnerabilities influence the SoE attack risk of management defeats in organizations, and the SoE attack risk of unexpected changes in management and the SoE attack risk of digital evidence influence risk management practices. Finally, risk management practices influence organizational activities. Cronbach's alpha coefficient was used to test the reliability of the pilot survey items. A coefficient value closer to "1" was needed. Table 3.6 The results of the reliability test.

Table 3.5: Organizational activity reliability test.

Organizational Activities	Items	Cronbach's Alpha value	N
OrganizationalActivities	6	0.833	30

Note: Items – Numbers of variables, N –Total Number of Respondents

3.6. Empirical Study

Based on the questionnaire survey, an empirical study is eminently suited for investigating SoE attack risks and the risk management practices for preventing SoE attacks in organizations. Analysis of the data was conducted using Smart PLS 4, which led to the following conclusions. The explanations of the research approach and results of the empirical study phase are summarized in Table 3.6.

Table 3.6: The empirical phase research approach

Input	Research Approach (Process)	Results (Output)
Refined Questionnaire	Distributed to 384 samplepopulation by using purposive sampling	143 – respondent data validfor data analysis.
Valid data- for Analysis	Conduct an appropriatestatistical analysis.	SoE attacking risks rankingin the organization. SoE attacking risks analysis. Risk management practices for the prevention techniqueof SoE attacks.

Primary data collection was conducted via the refined questionnaire. Selection of the 384- population sample was performed through the purposive sampling technique. This generated 143 – respondent data points to be analyzed to determine demographic information, SoE attack risk, and current risk management practices for preventing SoE attacks in organizations. A five- point Likert scale was used to measure these constructs. Additionally, the respondents' demographic profiles provided information on their personal working experience, risk of contracting SoE, etc. Appropriate statistical analysis techniques (such as 1) assessment of measurements (outer model) or 2 assessment of structural models (inner model) were deployed to assist in understanding the data characteristics.

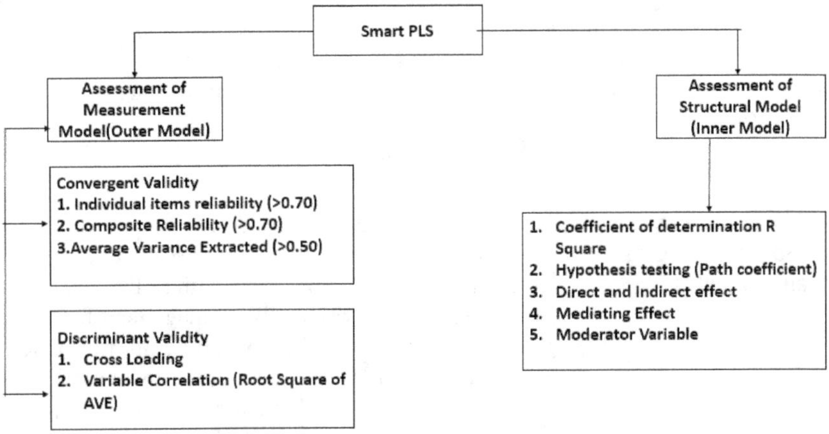

Figure 3.4: Data analysis using SmartPLS.

Figure 3.5 Data analysis using SmartPLs

The selection of the statistical analysis techniques was based on their ability to produce reliable and valid results. At the end of this phase, the researcher was able to analyze current risk management practices for preventing SoE attacks. Furthermore, the technique enabled the researcher to examine and explain the relationships among the variables in the study, as shown in Chapter 4 (Empirical Analysis and Discussion). To obtain a clearer picture of how the empirical analysis was conducted in this study.

Table 3.7: Illustrates the empirical roadmap and analysis technique used to answer the research questions and realize the research objectives.

Research Questions	Statistical Analysis Techniques	Research Objectives
What is the results for descriptive analysis of the study?	Use of percentages and frequency data to describe respondent's demographics and organization activities.	Research Objective 1: To identify various SoE attacking risks.

Research Questions	Statistical Analysis Techniques	Research Objectives
What are the ranking of critical SoE attacking risksitems in the organizations?	Use Mean Score to rank SoE attacking risks criticalness.	Research Objective 2 To analyze SoE attacking risks in various organization.
What are the significant characteristics associated with SoE attacking risks inthe organizations?	Use Assessment of Measurement Model test for association among various SoE attacking risksin the organization. (H1- H6)	Research Objective 2 To analyze SoE attacking risks in various organization.
What are the component of SoE attacking risk management?	Use Assessment of Structural Model test for association between SoE attacking risks and risk management practices for SoE attacks. (H6-H7)	Research Objective 3 To integrate SoE attacking risks with SoE attacking risk management for developing of information security framework for theprevention technique of SoE attacks.
What are the relationship of SoE attacking risk with Organizational Activities?	Use Assessment of Structural Model test for association between SoE attacking risk of digital evidence and risk management practices. (H6- H7)	Research Objective 2 To analyze SoE attacking risks in various organization.
What are the relationship ofrisk management practice with Organizational Activities?	Use Assessment of Structural Model test for association between SoE attacking risk managementand organizational activities. (H8-H9)	Objective 3: To integrate SoE attackingrisks with SoE attacking risk management for developing of information security framework for theprevention technique of SoE attacks.

3.7. Conceptual Framework

The conceptual framework was developed to conduct this study. These conceptual frameworks were developed to answer the research question and satisfy research objective 1 (identifying various SoE attack risks). Moreover, a conceptual framework was developed to satisfy research objective 2 (to analyze risk management practices for preventing SoE attacks in organizations) and objective 3 (to integrate SoE attack risks with SoE attack risk management to develop an information security framework for preventing SoE attacks). Detailed explanations ofthese research models are provided in the following section.

The conceptual framework shown in Figure 3.6 was built based on a combination of several past studies as a single research model. Based on this conceptual framework, the researcher determined the most relevant basic idea of the framework. As previously described, reliability tests were also conducted for items associated with SoE attack risk. There were ten (10) SoE attack risks of threats and twelve (12) SoE attack risks of vulnerabilities, whereas the SoE attack risk of threats and the SoE attack risk of vulnerabilities influenced seven (7) SoE attack risks of management defeats in organizations. However, this conceptual framework is useful for preventing SoE attacks in organizations. The conceptual framework considers the previous literature for managing SoE attacking risks, thus making it more reliable since it is also supported by theoretical perspectives and generic practices of managing such risks. The conceptual framework comprises a range of processes and activities (as shown in Figure 3.6), covering the entire spectrum of three stages (Stage 1: SoE attack risk of Preliminary Study Stage II: SoE attack risk evaluation and planning Stage III: SoE attack risk monitoring and control execution plan). As such, it is a specific tool for improving the efficacy of the entire SoE attack risk management process for the organization.

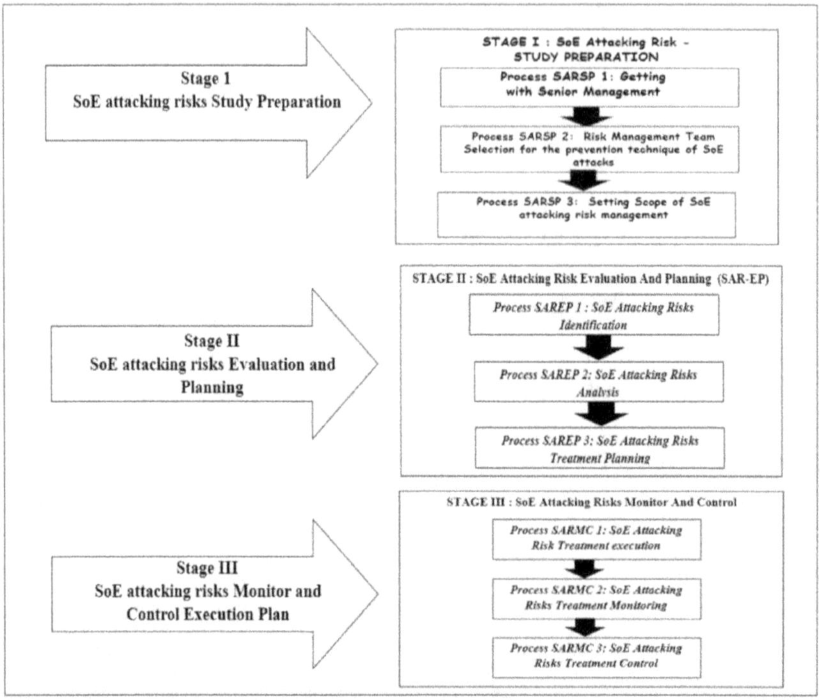

Figure 3.5: Conceptual framework diagram of SoE attacks and prevention techniques in risk management-based solutions for organizations.

Essentially, the conceptual framework for SoE attack risk management for an organization consists of these main stages. Each stage consists of several processes and activities. To highlight the contributions of this study, different notations were used to represent the processes and activities involved in the framework. The highlighted areas indicate the original contributions, while the dotted boxes indicate the partial contributions of the processes. Details about the framework components and contributions are discussed further later in the framework stage section. The SoE attack risks of threats, vulnerabilities, management defects in the organization, unexpected changes in management and digital evidence constructs and their respective items were as described in Chapter 2 and were used for exploratory factor analysis (EFA). A principal component analysis (PCA) was conducted on 42 items that were used for orthogonal rotation (varimax). For the purpose of this study, Factor loadings >0.4 were considered acceptable items relevant to the identified factors. Finally, the Cronbach's alpha coefficient was used to test the reliability of each identified item. The factor analysis produced the expected results of KMO and Bartlett's Test test, rotation of the sums squared loading, and rotation of the component matrix to establish research objective 2 (to analyze SoE attack risks in various organizations). Additionally, mean scores for the critical level of each SoE attack risk item were also calculated. The detailed results and discussion are presented in Chapter 4 (Analysis and Discussion).

A construct is a variable that is not directly observed, therefore, a measurement model is needed for each construct. In this research model, seven constructs (Vul, Thr, Mgt_d, Unxch, DE, R_M_P, and Org_Act) were measured by multiple items. All seven constructs are represented by arrows pointing from the construct to the indicators indicating a reflective measurement model. Each of these constructs is measured by multiple indicators. For instance, the endogenous construct Vul is measured by Vul1, Vul2 ......Vul12. In this case, the researcher developed the following hypothesis for path relationships:

H1: The risk of vulnerability to SoE attacks will have a significant effect on the risk of management defects in an organization.

H2: The risk of vulnerability to SoE attacks will have a significant effect on the risk of digital evidence being stolen.

H3: The risk of the SoE attacking a threat will have a significant effect on the risk of the SoEattacking management defects in the organization.

H4: The risk of an SoE attacking a threat will have a significant effect on the risk of an SoEattacking digital evidence.

H5: The risk of management defects in an organization being attacked by SoE will have asignificant effect on the risk of unexpected changes in management.

H6: The risk of the SoE attacking an unexpected change in management will have a significanteffect on the risk of the SoE attacking digital evidence.

H7: The risk of digital evidence attacking the SoE will have a significant effect on riskmanagement practices for preventing SoE attacks.

H8: The risk of the SoE attacking digital evidence will have a significant effect on OAs.

H9: Risk management practices for preventing SoE attacks will have a significant effect onorganizational activities.

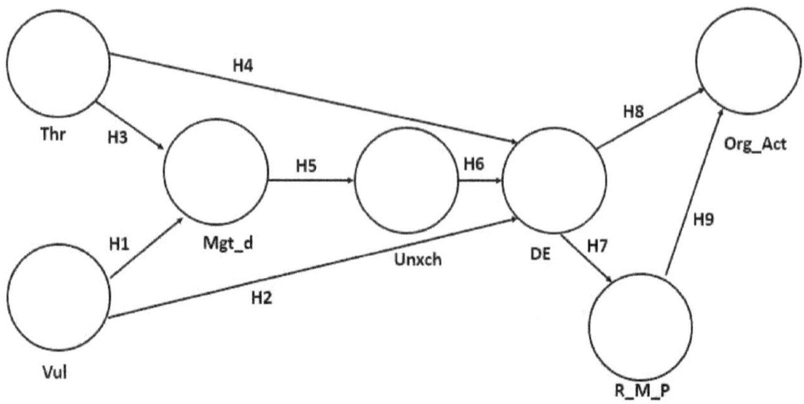

Figure 3.6: Diagram showing the hypothesized relationships

The results of these hypothesis tests are discussed in chapter 4 (Empirical analysis and discussion). The purpose of the hypothesis was to understand whether risk management practices are important for preventing SoE attacks in organizations. The results of these hypothesis tests are discussed further in Chapter 4 (Empirical Analysis and discussion). Statistical analysis was used to test the associations among the variables. The descriptive analysis was a part of the empirical analysis. The survey was administered on SoE attack risk items, such as the mean score and percentage, which were used to describe the level of risk of the SoE attack in the organizations. However, detailed descriptive results are discussed further in Chapter 4 (Empirical Analysis and Discussion). As part of the empirical analysis, descriptive analysis was performed for risk management practices for preventing SoE attacks. The mean score and percentage were used to describe the level at which Malaysian organizations practice risk management for preventing SoE attacks. The details of the descriptive analysis results are discussed in Chapter 4 (Empirical analysis and discussion).

3.8. Exploratory Study

In the exploratory study phase, semi structured interviews were conducted with focus groups from eight (8) organizations. Questionnaires were distributed to the organization to investigate the wideexperience with risk management practices for preventing SoE attacks. Then, comparisons were made among the organizations via a semi- structured approach with a questionnaire.

Table 3.8: Detailed explanations of the input, research approach and output in the exploratory studyphase

Input	Study Approach (Process)	Results (Output)
Semi structured way was used.	Content Analysis of semi structured way to reveal information. Identify theme of risk management practices for the prevention technique of SoE attacks.	Confirm existing risk factor for SoE attacks. Theme of risk management practices for the prevention technique of SoE attacks.
Conceptual study results, empirical study results, related documents or reports, past literature, current or best practices.	Compare result of focus group of semi structured way with empirical and conceptual study supportedwith literature. Identify similar and contradictory practices fromempirical results and exploratory study results.	High – level risk management for the prevention technique of SoE attacks in the framework component.

The purpose of the semi structured approach was to further explore risk management practices for preventing SoE attacks in the organizations. A semi-structured way to gain deeper insight into organizational practices of risk management for SoE attacks. The findings on their similarities or differences were compared with the results from previous empirical studies as well as related issues and challenges. Three categories of nominal scales were used as indicators to classify the practices of risk management in the organization. The nominal scale ranged from (Y), which refers to YES for the activities in which the task was conducted or was sometimes not conducted; (N), which refers to NO for the activities or tasks never conducted; and 'partial practice,' which refers to activities that were partially conducted. An exploratory study covered several components of risk management practices on how these eight (8) organizations identify, analyze, plan, monitor and control the risks of SoE attacks. The purpose of this exploratory study was to determine the high-level framework component of risk management for preventing SoE attacks as a basis for the initial framework. The detailed results of the exploratory findings will be discussed in chapter 5 (Exploratory Analysis and Results).

3.9. Framework Development

In the framework development phase, the conceptual study, empirical study and exploratory study results were used as a basis for developing the risk management framework for the prevention technique of SoE attacks with detailed components. Related work was also developed to improve the understanding of each detailed component of the framework.

Table 3.9: Framework development phase: Research approach

Input	**Study Approach (process)**	**Results (components of the output)**
SoE attacking risk factors and risk management practice for the prevention technique of SoE attacks in the organizations.	Content Analysis of resultsin previous study phases.	ined High-level Framework.
Refined High-level Framework from previous phases	Synthesize results of previous phases.	Proposed framework. Draft of the proposed framework.
	Develop flow of practices managing SoE attacking risk in the organizations. Develop flow and steps managing SoE attacking risk in the organizations. Develop recommended worksheet that can be used together with the framework.	Proposed framework user manual. Recommended related worksheets for use in the proposed framework.

Both empirical and exploratory findings were used to provide supportive evidence to refine the high-level framework components. The results of the empirical analysis were used to complement the exploratory analysis results on current practices of risk management for the prevention technique of SoE attacks in organizations. As a result, core components were identified for the development of the risk management framework. In addition, empirical and exploratory findings and guidelines were used as supplementary references to ensure the operability of the proposed framework in local and global communities. The detailed results of the proposed framework findings are discussed further in chapter 6 (Information Security Risk Management Framework for the Prevention Technique of SoE Attacks in Organizations). The proposed framework will be verified via an expert judgment approach, thus enhancing the acceptability of the framework for the industry and research community.

Table 3.10: Confirmatory phase study approach.

Input	Study Approach	Results (Output)
Related Documents, literature articles, proposed framework.	Review previous phasesresults. Review and compare related documents. Assess past findings.	Verify framework withexpert.
Proposed framework, Expert Knowledge and experiences.	In depth semi structured way was used with experts (expert judgment. Compile results of expert judgment (comments/ recommendations).	Validated framework.

An experienced expert in the field of information security, management and practitioners was identified for the confirmatory study. Based on the empirical and exploratory study, organizations that were actively involved in these activities were considered the best subjects of the confirmatory study. For the purpose of this study, face validity was assessed through expert judgments. The expert judgment method has been defined as an expression of opinion, based on knowledge and experience, which makes the framework more reliable and user friendly inside organizations. Specifically, expert judgment represents a more reliable framework for preventing SoE attacks. In addition, expert judgments are expert states of knowledge. aggregating opinions to cover a broad range of issues regarding a topic is a frequent process of accessing panel comments. Researchers have used expert judgment for many years across a variety of disciplines.

Specifically, the use of an expert helps to incorporate experience and study results when models of the processes involved are incomplete or when there is no consensus as to the correct model to apply. Ensuring expert judgment depends on the expert's knowledge, experience and motivation a between the expert and analyst. However, the main reason for adopting the expert judgment method in this study was to complete, validate, interpret and integrate the findings to confirm the acceptability of the framework. The method was also used to determine the present state of Knowledge in managing SoE attack risks in organizations suggests that expert judgment is commonly used when studies are completing, validating and interpreting existing data that assess the impact of a change and predicting the occurrence of future events and the consequences of a decision. The present state of knowledge in one field is determined, and the elements needed for decision-making are provided in the presence of several options. Similarly, well known researchers, as pioneers, have applied expert judgment for organizing and conducting their research successfully Herman Kahn, regarded as the father of scenario analysis, defines scenarios as hypothetical sequences of events constructed for the purpose of focusing attention on casual processes and decision- points. Expert judgment was also practice in the Delphi method to accomplish the research findings. The Delphi method was developed by the RAND Corporation in the early 1950s as a spinoff for air force-sponsored research. The original research was designed to anticipate the optimal targeting of U.S. industries by a hypothetical Soviet strategic planner. In the middle of the 1960s and early 1970s, the Delphi method was used in a wide variety of applications, and by 1974, the number of Delphi studies exceeded 10,000. The Delphi method has undergone substantial evolution and diversification. The Delphi method was most popular among engineers, research managers, policy analysts, and corporate planners in the late 1960s and early 1970s. By the middle of the 1970s, psychometrical, staff trained in conducting controlled experiments with humans, began taking serious interest in the Delphi methods and results. Moreover, numerous researchers have also used expert judgment for many years across a variety of disciplines and research works. For the above reasons, a similar method of expert judgment was adopted for this study. A review of various methods of expert judgment adopted by previous researchers revealed that a generic phase of expert judgment had been developed and was deemed suitable for the needs of this study (framework confirmatory study). Figure 3.7 illustrates the use of the generic expert judgment method to verify and validate the risk management framework for preventing SoE attacks in the organizations in this study. The results of the expert judgment of the framework and how the method was adopted for this study are discussed in detail in Chapter 7 (Framework Expert Judgment Confirmatory).

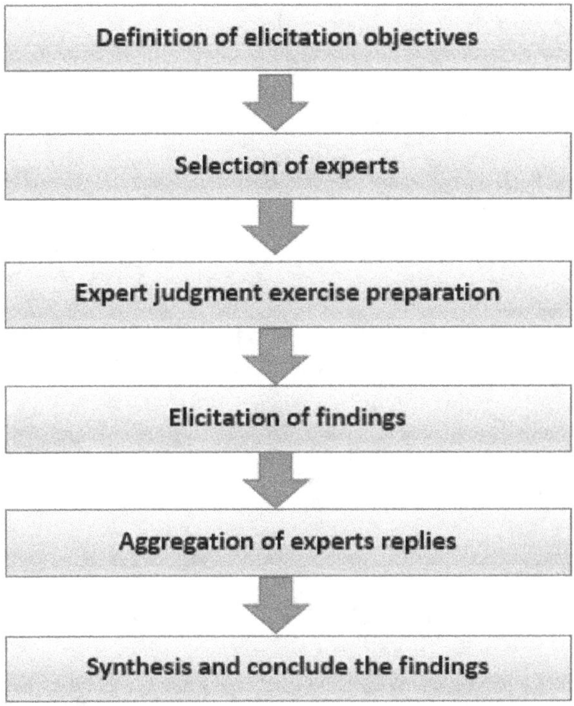

Figure 3.7: Generic Expert Judgment Methods

Chapter Four

Framework Alongside the Risk Management:"analyze SoE attack risks"

4.1. Data Analysis Strategies

The authors reported on the data analysis and evaluated the results according to two research objectives: (1) to identify various SoE attack risks and (2) to analyze the SoE attack risks in various organizations. The analysis and discussion are presented in two parts. First, the chapter provides a descript summary of the demographic profile data, focusing on the presentation of percentage frequencies. Second, this chapter reports on the exploratory SoE attack risks conducted to achieve objectives 1 and 2. Specifically, the latter part focuses on the analysis and discussion of empirical findings on SoE attack risks and SoE attack risk management in organizations. This second section also analyses and discusses findings on organizational activities and implementing risk management practices for the prevention technique of SoE attacks and how SoE attacks influence risk management for the prevention technique of SoE attacks in the organization. These empirical findings provide the basis for identifying the appropriate components in the information security risk management framework for preventing SoE attacks in organizations. The data were collected from the four organizations. The departments included education sectors, the health care sector, and banking and government agencies. It was difficult to determine the exact number of people who were working in that organization. Therefore, it was assumed that the sample size was infinite. There are various software packages, such as G*Power, or Excel, available, used to calculate the infinite sample size from the population. However, the sample size was calculated to be 384. Therefore, 384 questionnaires were distributed across the four sectors, and 143 responses were collected—a 37% response rate—which was sufficient for the analysis.

4.2. Descriptive analysis

Through purposive sampling, questionnaires were distributed to 384 respondents in various organizations, such as healthcare, education, banking and government agencies, who were directly involved in information and communication technology activities inside the organization. A total of 37% of the respondents (143 respondents) responded to the survey, and the following section provides a descriptive analysis of the respondents' demographic profiles obtained from the survey. The demographic profile revealed some salient points. The demographic data were collected from various organizations, such as banking sectors, healthcare sectors, education sectors and government agencies. All the organizations had similar responses for example, government agencies had 18% of the responses, healthcare had 24% of the responses, education sectors had 32% of the responses and banking sectors had 25%. However, the response rate was 55% for males and 44% for females. On the other hand, 25% of the respondents were >50 years old, 30% were between 46- and 50 years old, and 36 and 40 years old were 24%, 31% were between 31 and 35 years, and 33% were between 26 and 30 years. However, 29% of the participants had between 5 and 20 years of personal working experience, 32% had 4 years of working experience, and 19% had between 15 and 20 years of working experience was 34%. However, regarding their experience with SoE attacks, 57% of the respondents were about suspicious mail or unexpected calls, 42% had shown such experiences, and none had shown this type of experience. Regarding unexpected mail, 36% had not obtained any of these types, whereas 63% had this experience. Questionnaires were asked whether employees noticed any unauthorized persons without proper IDs working in the organization. A total of 17% of the respondents had never seen any type of people, but 23% had this type of experience. Informally, 18% of the participants said that the number was blocked, 22% said that the call was cancelled, 18% said that the email was deleted, 18% said that the contract with a security expert was signed and 27% said that the number was blocked.

Table 4.1: Shows the results

Organizational name	f	Rel f	Cf	Percentile
Governmentagencies	26	0.18	143	100
Healthcare	35	0.24	117	81.33

Organizational name	f	Rel f	Cf	Percentile
Education	46	0.32	82	57.15
Banking	36	0.25	36	25.27
Total	*143*			
Gender	**f**	**Rel f**	**Cf**	**Percentile**
Female	63	0.44	143	100
Male	80	0.55	80	55.94
Total	*143*			
Age	**f**	**Rel f**	**Cf**	**Percentile**
>50 years	25	0.17	143	100
46- 50 years	30	0.20	118	82.51
36- 40 years	24	0.16	88	61.53
31-35 years	31	0.21	64	44.75
26-30 years	33	0.23	33	23.07
Total	*143*			
Personal workingexperience	**f**	**Rel f**	**Cf**	**Percentile**
> 20 years	29	0.20	143	100
15-20 years	19	0.13	114	79.72
11-15 years	34	0.23	95	66.43
5 years	32	0.22	61	42.65
4 years	29	0.20	29	20.27
Total	*143*			
Experience of SoE attacks_1	**f**	**Rel f**	**cf**	**Percentile**
No	61	0.42	143	100
Yes	82	0.57	82	57.34
Total	*143*			
Experience of SoE attacks_2	**f**	**Rel f**	**cf**	**Percentile**
No	71	0.49	143	100
Yes	72	0.50	72	57.11
Total	*143*			
Experience of SoE attacks_3	**f**	**Rel f**	**cf**	**Percentile**
No	51	0.35	143	100
Yes	92	0.69	92	64.33
Total	*143*			
Experience of SoE attacks_3	**f**	**Rel f**	**cf**	**Percentile**
Block the mail	25	0.17	143	100
Contract withsecurity expert	34	0.23	118	82.51
Delete the mail	26	0.18	84	58.74

Experience of SoE attacks_3	f	Rel f	cf	Percentile
Cancel the call	26	0.22	58	40.55
Block thenumber	26	0.18	26	18.18
Total	*143*			

The level of SoE attack risk ranking and the questionnaire was administered to various organizations. The purpose is to determine the highest value of the ranking, to identify the highest SoE attack risk in the organization, which is relevant to research objective 2.

However, the SoE attack risks consist of

-SoE attacking risks of threats.
-SoE attack risks of vulnerabilities.
-SoE attacks the risks of management defects in the organization.
-SoE attacks the risks of unexpected change in management.
-SoE attacking risks of Digital Evidence.

The questionnaires were prepared according to the abovementioned SoE attack risks and distributed it among various organizations. Beyond the principle of basic security, the concept of SoE attacking risks of threats is the most complex part of SoE attacking risks. From the previous literature review, journal and other sources of book and scholarly articles, the following conclusions can be drawn: (10) The risk of the threat being identified is an example of an SoE attack. The questionnaires were distributed to several organizations to determine the ranking of the risk of the SoE attacking threats in the organization.

Table 4.2: SoE attack risk ranking of threats

SoE attacking risks of threats	Mean	Standard Deviation	No. of ranking
Loss, damage or destruction of digital evidence in the organization	3.18	1.328	1
Information leakage(extraction of loss of valuable or private information	3.00	1.554	2
Widespread unauthorized and uncontrolled used ofportable device and transportable computer media	2.91	1.375	3
Unauthorized accessor modification or disclosure of digital evidence.	2.91	1.446	3

SoE attacking risks of threats	Mean	Standard Deviation	No. of ranking
System error andfailure	2.82	1.401	4
Unauthorized exploitation of intellectual property(IP) example: plagiarism etc.	2.82	1.401	4
Poor SoE attacking risk detectionstudies	2.82	1.471	5
Identify theft ofpersonal data orinformation	2.73	1.421	6
Exploit other control weakness involving printed orother information rather than computer data and system.	2.55	1.368	7
Directly exploit control weakness inthe system	2.38	1.433	8

The vulnerability of SoE attacks refers to the weakness of safeguards in assets that make the system more harmful. The previous literature review, journal and other sources of book and scholarly articles reveal the following: (12) The authors identify the risk of attack on vulnerabilities. These questionnaires can be distributed to several organizations to determine the ranking of SoE attack risks of vulnerabilities in organizations.

Table 4.3: SoE attack risk ranking of vulnerabilities

SoE attacking risks of vulnerability	Mean	Standard Deviation	No. ofranking
The process of identifying and preserving digitalevidence in a manner that is legally acceptable	3.45	1.368	1
Complexity ofinformation technology and system	3.36	1.502	2
Lack of suitable control of digital evidence accessibility	3.27	1.348	3
Insufficient enforcement of law	3.17	1.421	3
The process of identifying and preserving digitalevidence in a manner that is legally acceptable	3.18	1.537	4
Insufficient backup	3.00	1.549	5
Inadequate investment in appropriate SoE attacking risk control	2.91	1.446	6
Lack of assets inventory management	2.91	1.446	6
User system accounts not in use	2.82	1.401	7
Disgruntled of organizational staff	2.61	1.401	7

SoE attacking risks of vulnerability	Mean	Standard Deviation	No. of ranking
Unreliable level ofdigital evidence protection	2.64	1.502	8

A breach of security occurs when stated organizational policies require an information security framework for the prevention technique of SoE attacks, whereas there are management defects in the organization. SoE activities are activities in which the attacker can perform bypass attacks if there are any management defects or unawareness of the organization. Therefore, identifying these issues is necessary for building a framework for preventing SoE attacks. A reviewof the previous literature and a review, of other scholarly articles revealed seven (7) SoE attack risks of management defects in the organization. The questionnaires were distributed to several organizations to determine the ranking of the risk of the SoE attacking management defects in theorganization.

Table 4.4: SoE attack risk ranking of management defects in the organization

SoE attacking risksof management defects in the organization	Mean	Standard Deviation	No. of ranking
Lack of suitable management and control over the user password	3.45	1.368	1
Disgruntled of service provider staff	3.27	1.489	2
Service provider exploitation control weakness in the process	3.27	1.555	2
Unaddressed serviceprovider's responsibility for the information security and confidentiality in contract	3.09	1.446	3
Staff negligent of service provider such as programmertechnical architecture, tester and manager	3.09	1.375	3
Disgruntled or untrained or ignorant employeewho make genuine human error	2.91	1.541	4
Unorganized accesscontrol and privilege on user application accounts	2.91	1.445	4

An element that contributes to SoE attack risk is unexpected change in management. Unexpected change in management refers to rapid change in the organization in which employees sometimes feel difficult to adopt and that happens by a service provider. This approach is another way to increase the ease with which SoE attackers to attack in the organization. However, from the previous literature studies and various scholarly articles, there were nine (9) SoE attack risks of unexpected change in an organization.

Table 4.5: Ranking of unexpected changes in management risk due to SoE attacks

SoE attacking riskof unexpected change in management	Mean	Standard Deviation	No. of ranking
Lack of security training and awareness regarding SoE attacks	3.73	1.272	1
Directly exploit control weakness in the system	3.64	1.286	2
Insufficient attention to human factors of SoE attacks in design implementation	3.45	1.214	3
Lack of digital evidence owners responsibility	3.45	1.368	3
Lack of business continuity plan management	3.18	1.328	4
Unethical competitors (trade secrets, customer list etc)	3.18	1.250	4
Frequently change in business policies	3.00	1.265	5
Loss of confidentiality of classification information	2.91	1.544	6
Severely affect the business survivability of organization	2.91	1.446	6

As described in the previous section, risk has been assessed in a variety of fields, such as insurance, economics, management, medicine, operation research and engineering. However, in the information security domain, SoE attacks are one kind of bypass attack. The intruder is interested only in digital files and folder. Digital files and folder refer to important documents for any organization. Hence, missing this document by SoE attacks is a very harmful matter for any organization. However, digital evidence must be preserved according to the Evidence Act. Therefore, digital evidence is one of the risks of SoE attacks in organizations. The questionnaires were distributed to several organizations to determine the ranking of SoE attack risks of digital evidence in organizations.

Table 4.6: SoE attack risk ranking of digital evidence

SoE attacking risk of digital evidence	Mean	Standard Deviation	No. of ranking
Digital Evidence must be preservedand hold up according in courtof Evidence Act.	3.73	1.009	1
Digital Evidence perception for risk management importance for SoE attacking riskcontrol	3.73	1.191	1
Digital documentation ofpolicy and procedure	3.55	1.440	2
Legal activity anddocumentation	3.41	1.211	3
Organizationalperception of Evidence Act.	3.38	1.192	4
Organization policy of employee onlineinformation update	3.37	1.746	5

4.3. Reflective Measurement Analysis for the Study Model

The path model was prepared for the study model. This approach would demonstrate the relationships and hypotheses of the variables that have already been described. However, in this study the term construct is used to describe a variable that was not directly measured by indicators; for that reason, it was referred to as a latent variable. However, in this study, a conceptual model for SoE attacks and prevention techniques in digital evidence -based solutions was developed in Chapter 3 on two theories :1) Structural theories specify how constructs are related to each other in the structural model. The sequence and location of the construct were based on the theory observed by the researcher. However, latent variables that act only as independent variables are called exogenous latent variables. 2) As described in chapter 3, the measurement research model specifies the relationships between the constructs and the indicators. However, in this study, some variable constructs were not directly observed. Therefore, a measurement model was needed for each construct. In this model, seven constructs (Vul, Thr, Mgt_d, Unxch, DE, R_M_P, and Org_Act) were measured by multiple items, as displayed in the figure.

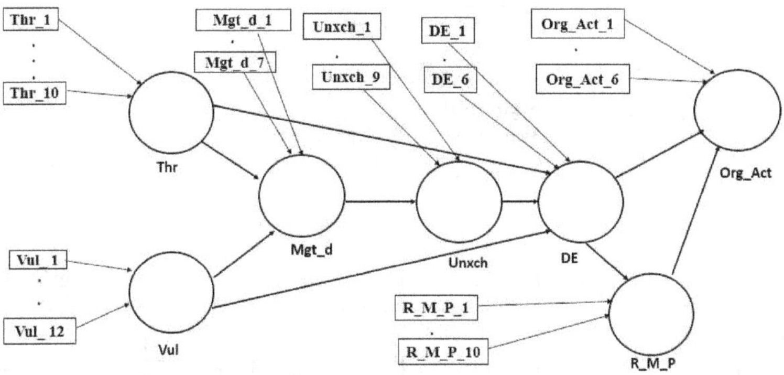

Figure 4.1: Model diagram with constructs and items related to SoE attacks and prevention techniques in digital evidence-based solutions for organizations

All seven constructs have arrows pointing from the construct to the indicators to indicatea reflective measurement model. Each of these constructs was measured by multiple indicators. For instance, the endogenous construct vulnerabilities were measured by Vul1, Vul2…Vul12 andas were other constructs. The results Summary of reflective measurements for the model.

Table 4.7: Reflective measurement for the model

Latent variable	Indicator	Internal consistency		Convergent Validity		Discriminant validity	
		Composite Reliability	Cronbach Alpha	Loading	AVE		
		0.6-0.9	0.6-0.9	>0.7		>0.5	HTMT confidence interval does not include 1
SoE Attacking Risk of Threats	Thr1	0.940	0.928	0.639		0.613	Yes
	Thr2			0.880			
	Thr3			0.803			
	Thr4			0.860			
	Thr5			0.651			
	Thr6			0.836			
	Thr7			0.878			
	Thr8			0.863			
	Thr9			0.741			
	Thr10			0.617			

Latent variable	Indicator	Internal consistency		Convergent Validity		Discriminant validity	
		Composite Reliability	Cronbach Alpha	Loading	AVE		
		0.6-0.9	**0.6-0.9**	**>0.7**		**>0.5**	**HTMT confidence interval does not include 1**
SoE Attacking Risk of Vulnerabilities	Vul1	0.966	0.962	0.784		0.707	Yes
	Vul2			0.766			
	Vul3			0.689			
	Vul4			0.857			
	Vul5			0.905			
	Vul6			0.924			
	Vul7			0.854			
	Vul8			0.837			
	Vul9			0.876			
	Vul10			0.858			
	Vul11			0.915			
	Vul12			0.792			
SoE Attacking Risk of Management Defects in the organization	Mgt_d1	0.920	0.897	0.853		0.625 0.625	Yes
	Mgt_d2			0.829			
	Mgt_d3			0.861			
	Mgt_d4			0.674			
	Mgt_d5			0.790			
	Mgt_d6			0.623			
	Mgt_d7			0.867			
	Unxch1	0.935	0.921	0.624		0.616	Yes
SoE Attacking Risk of Unexpected change in management	Unxch2			0.864			
	Unxch3			0.804			
	Unxch4			0.729			
	Unxch5			0.797			
	Unxch6			0.764			
	Unxch7			0.825			
	Unxch8			0.815			
	Unxch9			0.814			

Latent variable	Indicator	Internal consistency		Convergent Validity		Discriminant validity	
		Composite Reliability	Cronbach Alpha	Loading	AVE		
		0.6-0.9	**0.6-0.9**	**>0.7**		**>0.5**	**HTMT confidence interval does not include 1**
SoE Attacking Risk of Digital Evidence	DE1	0.873	0.813	0.820		0.567	Yes
	DE2			0.819			
	DE3			0.865			
	DE4			0.863			
	DE5			0.783			
	DE6			0.110			
Risk Management Practice for the prevention technique of SoE attacks	R_P_M1	0.973	0.962	0.181		0.792	Yes
	R_M_P2			0.965			
	R_M_P3			0.983			
	R_M_P4			0.919			
	R_M_P5			0.902			
	R_M_P6			0.927			
	R_M_P7			0.922			
	R_M_P8			0.911			
	R_M_P9			0.927			
	R_M_P10			0.965			
Organizational Activities	Org_Act1	0.962	0.925	0.968		0.810	Yes
	Org_Act2			0.895			
	Org_Act3			0.906			
	Org_Act4			0.936			
	Org_Act5			0.965			
	Org_Act6			0.699			

4.4. Significance and relevance of the formative indicator for the model

Another criterion for evaluating the formative measurement model was the significance and relevance of the participants' outer weight. The values of the outer weights express the contributions of each indicator to the construct. The estimated outer weights in formative measurements were often lower than the outer loading of the reflective indicator, because they were influenced by the other relationship is the construct of SoE attacks and prevention techniques in digital evidence -based solutions.

However, the t- values are used for the measurement of the structure of the research model relationship. Researchers could compare the t values with the critical values from the standard normal distribution to determine whether the coefficients of SoE attacks and prevention technique in digital evidence -based solutions were significantly different from zero. The critical value for a significance of 5% (alpha =0.05) probability of error was 1.96 (two -tailed) (Cohen., 1998). Researchers could obtain more detailed insights by reviewing the bootstrapping results after considering the final results.

Table 4.8: The bias -corrected confidence intervals

Formative Construct	*Formative Indicator*	*Outer weight*	*Outer loading*	*T-Statistics (O/STDEV)*	*P-value*	*95% Bca Confidence Interval*		*Significance (P<0.05)?*
SoE Attacking Risk of Threats	Thr1	0.090	0.639	9.257	0.000	0.496	0.751	Yes
	Thr2	0.144	0.617	31.784	0.000	0.818	0.925	Yes
	Thr3	0.125	0.880	20.786	0.000	0.723	0.870	Yes
	Thr4	0.146	0.860	29.786	0.000	0.773	0.905	Yes
	Thr5	0.092	0.651	9.129	0.000	0.492	0.773	Yes
	Thr6	0.136	0.836	26.651	0.000	0.749	0.883	Yes
	Thr7	0.150	0.878	31.991	0.000	0.800	0.919	Yes
	Thr8	0.147	0.863	30.255	0.000	0.783	0.907	Yes
	Thr9	0.126	0.741	12.664	0.000	0.614	0.840	Yes
	Thr10	0.990	0.617	8.254	0.000	0.441	0.739	Yes
SoE Attacking Risk of Vulnerabilities	Vul1	0.092	0.784	16.979	0.000	0.637	0.853	Yes
	Vul2	0.093	0.766	15.273	0.000	0.641	0.848	Yes
	Vul3	0.085	0.689	10.358	0.000	0.540	0.808	Yes
	Vul4	0.099	0.857	25.722	0.000	0.766	0.909	Yes
	Vul5	0.107	0.689	35.303	0.000	0.837	0.944	Yes
	Vul6	0.108	0.857	60.157	0.000	0.889	0.948	Yes

Formative Construct	*Formative Indicator*	*Outer weight*	*Outer loading*	*T-Statistics (O/STDEV)*	*P-value*	*95% Bca Confidence Interval*		*Significance (P<0.05)?*
SoE Attacking Risk of Vulnerabilities	Vul7	0.099	0.905	14.475	0.000	0.797	0.925	Yes
	Vul8	0.098	0.924	21.381	0.000	0.773	0.918	Yes
	Vul9	0.104	0.854	28.139	0.000	0.837	0.944	Yes
	Vul10	0.099	0.837	24.296	0.000	0.889	0.948	Yes
	Vul11	0.109	0.876	41.376	0.000	0.797	0.942	Yes
	Vul12	0.093	0.792	15.273	0.000	0.687	0.902	Yes
SoE Attacking Risk of Management defects in the organization	Mgt_d1	0.203	0.853	17.544	0.000	0.703	0.821	Yes
	Mgt_d2	0.198	0.825	27.609	0.000	0.797	0.887	Yes
	Mgt_d3	0.193	0.861	10.902	0.000	0.775	0.918	Yes
	Mgt_d4	0.175	0.790	15.642	0.000	0.588	0.917	Yes
	Mgt_d5	0.144	0.795	10.094	0.000	0.682	0.843	Yes
	Mgt_d6	0.196	0.623	28.828	0.000	0.770	0.812	Yes
	Mgt_d7	0.208	0.864	38.602	0.000	0.643	0.899	Yes
SoE Attacking Risk of Unexpected change in management	Unxch1	0.101	0.624	10.902	0.000	0.510	0.724	Yes
	Unxch2	0.163	0.864	36.635	0.000	0.817	0.904	Yes
	Unxch3	0.154	0.804	20.264	0.000	0.722	0.878	Yes
	Unxch4	0.120	0.729	11.808	0.000	0.594	0.839	Yes
	Unxch5	0.144	0.797	17.994	0.000	0.700	0.871	Yes
	Unxch6	0.142	0.825	15.805	0.000	0.650	0.850	Yes
	Unxch7	0.151	0.815	19.424	0.000	0.723	0.891	Yes
	Unxch8	0.142	0.811	21.382	0.000	0.730	0.882	Yes
	Unxch9	0.147	0.732	17.773	0.000	0.715	0.899	Yes
SoE Attacking Risk of Digital Evidence	DE1	0.240	0.820	15.013	0.000	0.685	0.899	Yes
	DE2	0.217	0.819	17.628	0.000	0.704	0.923	Yes
	DE3	0.243	0.865	25.844	0.000	0.792	0.921	Yes
	DE4	0.255	0.863	24.844	0.000	0.634	0.855	Yes
	DE5	0.256	0.748	12.812	0.000	0.679	0.790	Yes
	DE6	0.032	0.110	1.151	0.250	-0.079	0.257	No
Risk Management	R_M_P1	0.023	0.181	1.900	0.058	-0002	0.355	No
	R_M_P2	0.122	0.965	56.438	0.000	0.930	0.995	Yes
	R_M_P3	0.124	0.985	131.054	0.000	0.963	0.994	Yes
	R_M_P4	0.117	0.919	22.061	0.000	0.821	0.983	Yes
	R_M_P5	0.116	0.902	15.729	0.000	0.739	0.988	Yes
Practice for the prevention technique of SoE attacks	R_M_P6	0.117	0.927	28.799	0.000	0.860	0.983	Yes
	R_M_P7	0.119	0.922	22.645	0.000	0.840	0.943	Yes
	R_M_P8	0.113	0.911	25.295	0.000	0.750	0.890	Yes
	R_M_P9	0.115	0.927	26.925	0.000	0.833	0.945	Yes
	R_M_P10	0.121	0.965	52.483	0.000	0.844	0.980	Yes

Formative Construct	*Formative Indicator*	*Outer weight*	*Outer loading*	*T-Statistics (O/STDEV)*	*P-value*	*95% Bca Confidence Interval*		*Significance (P<0.05)?*
Organizational Activities	Org_Act1	0.207	0.968	89.729	0.000	0.924	0.984	Yes
	Org_Act2	0.176	0.895	22.222	0.000	0.808	0.905	Yes
	Org_Act3	0.187	0.906	29.921	0.000	0.841	0.943	Yes
	Org_Act4	0.194	0.936	36.500	0.000	0.871	0.958	Yes
	Org_Act5	0.199	0.965	72.874	0.000	0.932	0.984	Yes
	Org_Act6	0.141	0.699	13.189	0.000	0.594	0.806	Yes

This model estimates parameters with the purpose of maximizing the explained variance of the endogenous latent variables. The research model was evaluated in terms of how well it predicted the endogenous variables.

Table 4.9: Collinearity statistics (VIF):

	DE	Mgt_d	Org_Act	R_M_P	Thr	Unxch	Vul
DE			3.861	1.000			
Mgt_d						1.000	
Org_Act							
R_M_P			3.861				
Thr		4.311	3.581				
Unxch		2.949					
Vul		4.856	4.856				

All the VIF values were below the threshold of 5. Therefore, collinearity should be below the threshold of 5. Therefore, collinearity among the predictive constructs was not a critical issue in the structural model. A VIF higher than 5, indicates that the tolerance value was 0.2, indicating a potential collinearity problem, should consider removing one of the constructs, merging predictors or creating higher order constructs. The R2 was the most commonly used parameter for evaluating the structural model coefficient of determination. The coefficient represents the amount of variance in the endogenous constructs explained by all of the related exogenous constructs. This coefficient was calculated as the square correlation between a specific endogenous construct's actual and predicted values. The R -square value ranges from 0 to 1, with a higher score indicating higher levels of predictive accuracy.

Table 4.10: R2 values

	R – Square	R Square Adjusted
DE	0.937	0.936
Mgt_d	0.800	0.899
Unxch	0.861	0.868
R_M_P	0.741	0.740
Org_Act	0.862	0.860

In fact, the path coefficient for SoE attacks and prevention techniques in digital evidence-based solutions had standardized values between -1 and +1. A path coefficient close to +1 represents a strong positive relationship and is statistically significant. However, sometimes the path coefficient values are very low or close to 0 and are not significantly different from zero. The SoE attack risk of vulnerabilities (Vul) having a path effect on the SoE attack risk of management defects (Mgt_d) is 0.596. The SoE attack risk of vulnerabilities (Vul) having a path effect on the SoE attack risk of digital evidence (DE) would be (0.437). However, the risk of an SoE attacking a threat (Thr) having a path effect on the risk of an SoE attacking a management defect (Mgt_d) is 0.363). The risk of an SoE attacking a risk threat (Thr) having a path effect on the risk of an SoE attacking Digital Evidence (DE) would be (0.315). However, the risk of the SoE attack on management defects (Mgt_d) having a path effect on the risk of unexpected change in management (Unxch) would be (0.828). Hence, the SoE attack risk of unexpected change in management (Unxch) having a path effect on the SoE attack risk of digital evidence (DE) is 0.237. The SoE attack risk of digital evidence (DE) having a path effect on risk management practice for the prevention technique of SoE attacks (R_M_P) would be 0.861. The SoE attack risk of Digital Evidence (DE) having a path effect on Organizational Activities (Org_Act) would be (0.146). The risk management practice for preventing SoE attacks that have a path effect on organizational activities (Org_Act) would be 0.852. Whether the path coefficient for SoE attacks and prevention technique in digital evidence -based solutions was significant should be evaluated because the standard error can be obtained from bootstrapping. The bootstrapping standard error calculates the empirical t- value and p- value for all structural path coefficients. When an empirical t- value was larger than the critical value, it was concluded that the coefficient was statistically significant (at a certain error probability or significance level). The generally used critical value for the two-tailed test was 1.96 (significance level = 5%). Instead of reporting the t- value and p- value, it would also be suggested that the bootstrap confidence interval, be reported to indicate whether a path coefficient was significantly different from zero. The bootstrap confidence interval was based on standard error derived from bootstrapping and specifies that the range into which the true population parameter falls within a certain level of confidence interval of this research model would not include zero for an estimated path coefficient. The hypothesis that the path equals zero was rejected, and a significant effect was reached. When interpreting the results of the path model, the significance of all structural model relationships must be tested using the t value, p- value and bootstrapping confidence interval. Most researchers use the p value, which is equal to the probability of erroneously rejecting a true null hypothesis (assuming a significant path coefficient when it was not significant for the research model) when assuming a significance level of 5%, the p- value must be smaller than 0.05 to conclude that the relationship under consideration is significant at the 5% level. After analyzing the results at the 5% significance level, we found that the relationships in the structural model, (Vul) ->(Mgt_d), p(0.000), were significant, and (Vul)-> (DE), P(0.000) were significant, (Thr)->(Mgt_d), and p(0.000) were significant, (Thr)->(DE), and p(0.000),were significant, (Mgt_d)-> (Unxch),and p(0.000),were significant, (Unxch)->(DE),and p(0.000) were significant, (DE)->(R_M_P),and p(0.000) were significant, (DE)->(Org_Act), and p(0.000), were significant, and (R_M_P) ->(Org_Act),and p(0.000) were significant.

Table 4.11: Shows the path coefficients with t values and p values.

	Original Sample(O)	**Sample Mean (M)**	**Standard deviation (STDEV)**	**T-Statistics (O|STDEV)**	**P value**
Vul->Mgt_d	0.596	0.592	0.091	6.580	0.000
Vul->DE	0.437	0.433	0.098	4.480	0.000
Thr->Mgt_d	0.368	0.373	0.098	3.760	0.000
Thr->DE	0.315	0.319	0.094	3.351	0.000

	Original Sample(O)	Sample Mean (M)	Standard deviation (STDEV)	T-Statistics (O|STDEV)	P value
Mgt_d->Unxch	0.928	0.930	0.018	52.555	0.000
Unxch->DE	0.237	0.234	0.092	2.572	0.010
DE->R_M_P	0.861	0.859	0.034	4.307	0.000
DE->Org_Act	1.146	0.146	0.034	4.307	0.000
R_M_P->Org_Act	0.852	0.827	0.032	26.938	0.000

The table shows that the path coefficients are as follows: (Vul)-> (DE), (Vul)->(Mgt_d), (Unxch)->(DE), (Thr)->(Mgt_d), (R_M_P)->(Org_Act), (Mgt_d)->(Unxch), (DE)>(R_M_P), (DE)-> (R_M_P), (DE)-> (Org_Act) are significant for SoE attacks and prevention techniques in digital evidence - based solutions. The hypothesis that the path equals zero was rejected, if the confidence interval for an estimated path coefficient did not include zero, it would be assumed that the effect was significant. In other words, a null hypothesis (path coefficient zero), in the population was rejected at a given level α, if the corresponding (1-α) bootstrap confidence interval did not include zero or a significant effect.

Table 4.12: Confidence intervals

	Original Sample(O)	Sample Mean (M)	2.5%	97.5%
Vul->Mgt_d	0.596	0.592	0.417	0.772
Vul->DE	0.437	0.433	0.248	0.636
Thr->Mgt_d	0.368	0.373	0.168	0.546

	Original Sample(O)	**Sample Mean (M)**	**2.5%**	**97.5%**
Thr->DE	0.315	0.319	0.121	0.489
Mgt_d->Unxch	0.928	0.930	0.893	0.962
Unxch->DE	0.237	0.234	0.064	0.425
DE->R_M_P	0.861	0.859	0.787	0.915
DE->Org_Act	1.146	0.146	0.075	0.209
R_M_P->Org_Act	0.852	0.827	0.792	0.916

By observing at the significance level, we found that in the relationship (Vul)->(Mgt_d). For a probability error (significance level of 5%), the confidence interval has a lower bound of 0.417 and an upper bound of 0.772. Another observation revealed that (Vul)->(DE). For a probability error (significance level of 5%), the confidence interval has a lower bound of 0.248 and an upper bound of 0.636. Found that (Thr)->(Mgt_d), p (0.000), for a probability error (significance level of 5%), the confidence interval has a lower bound of 0.168 and an upper bound of 0.546. For (Thr)->(DE), p (0.000), for a probability error (significance level of 5%), the confidence interval has a lower bound of 0.121 and an upper bound of 0.489. For (Mgt_d)->(Unxch), p (0.000), for a probability error (significance, 5%), and a confidence interval error (significance level of 5%), the confidence intervals have a lower bound of 0.893 and an upper bound of 0.962. For (Unxch)->(DE), p (0.000), for a probability error (significance level of 5%), the confidence interval has a lower bound of 0.064 and an upper bound of 0.415. For (DE)->(R_M_P), p (0.000), for a probability error (significance level of 5%), the confidence interval has a lower bound of 0.787 and an upper bound of 0.915. For (DE)->(Org_Act), p (0.000), for a probability error (significance level of 5%), the confidence interval has a lower bound of 0.075 and an upper bound of 0.209. For (R_M_P) -> (Org_Act), for a probability error (significance level of 5%), the confidence interval has a lower bound of 0.792

and an upper bound of 0.916 above analysis revealed that all of the confidence intervals of the relationships did not all fall within zero. Based on the t- value, and p- value, we can summarize the hypothesis testing.

Table 4.13: Results of hypothesis testing

	Relationship between construct	t-value	p-value	ConfidenceInterval	Findings
H1	(Vul)->(Mgt_d)	6.580	0.000	(0.417-0.772)	H1 supported
H2	(Vul)->(DE)	4.480	0.000	(0.248-0.637)	H2 supported
H3	(Thr)->(Mgt_d)	3.760	0.000	(0.168-0.546)	H3 supported
H4	(Thr)->(DE)	3.351	0.001	(0.121-0.489)	H4 supported
H5	(Mgt_d)->(Unxch)	52.555	0.000	(0.893-0.962)	H5 supported
H6	(Unxch)->(DE)	2.572	0.000	(0.064-0.415)	H6 supported
H7	(DE)->(R_M_P)	25.932	0.000	(0.787-0.915)	H7 supported
H8	(DE)->(Org_Act)	4.307	0.000	(0.075-0.209)	H8 supported
H9	(R_M_P)->(Org_Act)	26.938	0.000	(0.792-0.916)	H9 supported

Note: - Significance at 0.05 (2-tailed)

The indirect effects of Thr on Mgt_d on Unxch were the product of the path coefficient (mediation path 1). Thr on Mgt_d on Unxch on DE were the product of the path coefficient of (mediation path 2);, Thr on DE on R_M_P were the path coefficient (mediation path 3);, Thr on Mgt_d on Unxch on DE on R_M_P were the path coefficient (mediation path 4), Thr on DE on Org_Act were the path coefficient of (mediation path 5), Thr on DE on R_M_P on Org_Act were the path coefficient (mediation path 6) and Thr on Mgt_d on Unxch on DE on R_M_P on Org_Act were the path coefficient (mediation path 7). Similarly, the indirect effects of Vul on Mgt_d on Unxch were products of the path coefficient (mediation path 1), Vul on Mgt_d on Unxch on DE were products of the path coefficient (mediation path 2), Vul on DE on R_M_P were the path coefficient (mediation path 3), Vul on Mgt_d on Unxch on DE on R_M_P were the path coefficient of (mediation path 4), Vul on DE on Org_Act were the path coefficient of (mediation path 5), and Vul on DE on R_M_P to Org_Act are the path coefficients (mediation path 6), and Vul to Mgt_d to Unxch to DE to R_M_P to Org_Act are the path coefficients (mediation path 7). However, Mgt_d to Unxch to DE were path coefficients of (mediation path 1), Mgt_d to Unxch to DE to R_M_P were path coefficients of (mediation path 2), Mgt_d to Unxch to DE to Org_Act were path coefficients of (mediation path 3), and Mgt_d to Unxch to DE to R_M_P to Org_Act were path coefficients of (mediation path 4). Whereas Unxch to DE to R_M_P were path coefficients of (mediation path 1), Unxch to DE to Org_Act were path coefficients of (mediation path 2), and Unxch to DE to R_M_P to Org_Act were path coefficients of (mediation path 3). Hence, DE to R_M_P to Org_Act were path coefficients of (mediation path 1). To test the significance of the indirect effect, the researcher used the bootstrap results.

Table 4.14: Shows the specific indirect effects.

	Original Sample(O)	**Sample Mean(M)**	**Standard Deviation (STDEV)**	**T Statistics**	**p – value**
Thr->Mgt_d->Unxch	0.342	0.346	0.094	3.616	0.000
Thr->Mgt_d->Unxch->DE	0.081	0.086	0.047	1.725	0.085
Thr->DE->R_M_P	0.271	0.277	0.085	3.192	0.002

	Original Sample(O)	**Sample Mean(M)**	**Standard Deviation (STDEV)**	**T Statistics**	**p – value**
Thr->Mgt_d->Unxch->DE->R_M_P	0.070	0.073	0.040	1.735	0.083
Thr->Mgt_d->Unxch->DE->Org_Act	0.012	0.013	0.007	1.587	0.113
Thr->DE->Org_Act	0.046	0.047	0.018	2.505	0.013
Thr->DE->R_M_P -> Org_Act	0.231	0.236	0.073	3.161	0.002
Thr->Mgt_d->Unxch->DE->R_M_P->Org_Act	0.059	0.063	0.034	1.730	0.084

	Original Sample(O)	Sample Mean(M)	Standard Deviation (STDEV)	T Statistics	p – value
Vul->Mgt_d->Unxch	0.553	0.552	0.084	6.606	0.000
Vul->Mgt_d->Unxch->DE	0.131	0.132	0.053	2.456	0.014
Vul->DE->R_M_P	0.376	0.366	0.088	4.276	0.000
Vul->Mgt_d->Unxch->DE->R_M_P->Org_Act	0.096	0.097	0.039	2.435	0.015
Vul->Mgt_d->Unxch->DE-->Org_Act	0.019	0.017	0.009	2.207	0.028
Vul->DE->Org_Chr	0.064	0.062	0.021	3.055	0.002

	Original Sample(O)	Sample Mean(M)	Standard Deviation (STDEV)	T Statistics	p – value
Vul->DE->R_M_P->Org_Act	0.320	0.312	0.075	4.235	0.000
Vul->Mgt_d->DE->R_M_P->Org_Act	0.096	0.097	0.039	2.435	0.015
Mgt_d->Unxch->DE	0.220	0.226	0.093	2.364	0.018
Mgt_d->Unxch->DE->R_M_P	0.189	0.193	0.080	2.375	0.018
Mgt_d_->Unxch->DE->Org_Act	0.032	0.033	0.015	2.106	0.036
Mgt_d->Unxch-	0.161	0.165	0.068	2.359	0.019

	Original Sample(O)	Sample Mean(M)	Standard Deviation (STDEV)	T Statistics	p – value
>DE- >R_M_P- >Org_Act					
Unxch- >DE- >R_M_P	0.204	0.207	0.084	2.419	0.016
Unxch- >DE- >Org_Act	0.035	0.033	0.016	2.141	0.033
Unxch- >DE- >R_M_P - >Org_Act	0.174	0.177	0.072	2.402	0.017
DE- >R_M_P- >Org_Act	0.733	0.738	0.040	18.413	0.000

After testing the indirect effect with a bootstrapping procedure, we similarly tested the significance of the direct effect on a path coefficient.

Table 4.15: Direct effect values.

	Original Sample(O)	Sample Mean(M)	Standard Deviation (STDEV)	T Statistics	p – value
Thr- >Mgt_d	0.368	0.370	0.108	3.396	0.001
Thr->DE	0.315	0.312	0.092	3.423	0.001

	Original Sample (O)	Sample Mean(M)	Standard Deviation (STDEV)	T Statistics	p–value
Vul->Mgt_d	0.596	0.598	0.102	5.864	0.000
Vul->DE	0.437	0.434	0.099	4.426	0.000
Mgt_d->Unxch	0.928	0.931	0.016	56.420	0.000
Unxch->DE	0.237	0.243	0.094	2.529	0.012
DE->R_M_P	0.861	0.863	0.033	26.278	0.000
DE->Org_Act	0.146	0.144	0.036	4.038	0.000
R_M_P->Org_Act	0.852	0.855	0.034	25.206	0.000

Table 4.16: Confidence interval bias corrected

	Original Sample(O)	**Sample Mean(M)**	**Bias**	**2.5%**	**97.5%**
Thr->Mgt_d	0.368	0.370	0.002	0.105	0.501
Thr->DE	0.315	0.312	-0.003	0.150	0.504
Vul->Mgt_d	0.596	0.598	-0.000	0.417	0.834
Vul->DE	0.437	0.434	-0.000	0.413	0.828
Mgt_d->Unxch	0.928	0.931	0.003	0.885	0.954
Unxch->DE	0.237	0.243	0.006	0.072	0.428
DE->R_M_P	0.861	0.863	0.002	0.769	0.912
DE->Org_Act	0.146	0.144	-0.003	0.078	0.226
R_M_P->Org_Act	0.852	0.855	0.003	0.777	0.914

Mediation implies a situation in which a third variable could explain the effect of the independent variable on the dependent variable better (Joseph F. et al., 2019). For example, in the SoE, attacks and prevention technique in a digital evidence -based solution model, the SoE attack risks such as the risk of the SoE attacking, threats, the risk of the SoE attacking vulnerability, the risk of the SoE attacking management defects, the risk of the SoE attacking unexpected change in management, and the risk of the SoE attacking digital evidence influenced by risk management practices for the prevention technique of SoE attacks (R_M_P) were endogenous latent variables that had dual relationships, both as independent and dependent relationships. This was the dependent construct because SoE attack risk influences risk management practices for the prevention technique of SoE attacks (R_M_P). Therefore, the risk management practice for the prevention technique of SoE attacks (R_M_P) was a possible mediator between SoE attack risks and Organizational Activities (Org_Act). The diagram shows the central factor in this model of specific effects with both constructs.

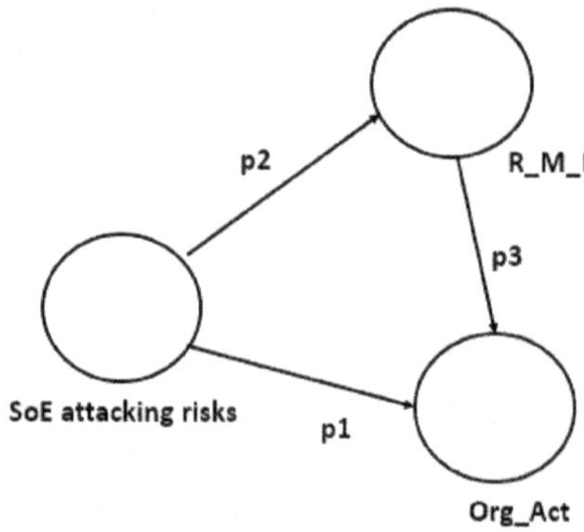

Figure 4.2: The mediating effect of the Model

In the diagram, the intervening process (mediating effect) is modeled as a risk management practice for the prevention technique of SoE attacks (R_M_P), and the other words, risk management practice (R_M_P) is a mediating variable. A change in the exogenous construct resulted in a change in the mediator variable, which in turn changed the endogenous construct. Direct effects were defined as the relationship connecting two constructs with a single arrow. Therefore, the direct effect p3 between SoE attack risks (such as Thr, Vul, Mgt_d, Unxch, DE) and Organizational Activities (Org_Act). Analyzing the strength of the mediating variable relationships with other constructs allowed the researcher to understand the cause. Effect relationship between an exogenous construct (Org_Act) and an endogenous construct (Vul, Thr, Mgt_d, Unxch, DE) and (R_M_P). According to Zhao, Lennch and Chen (2010), there are three types of mediation.: 1) complementary mediation, 2) competitive mediation, and 3) indirect mediation. For complementary mediation, both the indirect effect and direct effect were significant and pointed in the same direction. Conversely, competitive mediation occurs when the indirect effect and direct effect are significant but not in the opposite direction. The indirect effect was only mediation was when the indirect effect was significant, but the direct effect was not significant.

Table 4.17: The direct and indirect effects of SoE attacks and prevention techniques on digital evidence based solutions.

	direct effect	95% confidence intervalof direct effect	T-value	Sig. p<0.05?	Indirect effect	95% confidence interval effect	T-value	P – value	Indirect effect Sig.	Direct effect Sig.	Conclusion
Thr->Mgt_d->Unxch	0.368	(0.105-0.541)	3.396	0.001	0.342	(0.098-0.512)	3.325	0.001	Yes	Yes	Partial Mediation
Thr->Mgt_d->Unxch->DE	0.315	(0.143-0.501)	3.423	0.000	0.081	(0.017-0.183)	1.780	0.076	No	Yes	Full Mediation
Thr->DE->R_MP	0.861	(0.791-0.919)	26.278	0.000	0.271	(0.122-0.420)	3.415	0.001	Yes	Yes	Partial Mediation
Thr->Mgt_d->Unxch->DE->R_MP	0.237	(0.076-0.443)	2.529	0.012	0.070	(0.014-0.158)	1.771	0.077	No	Yes	Full Mediation
Thr->Mgt_d->Unxch	0.368	(0.105-0.541)	3.396	0.001	0.342	(0.098-0.512)	3.325	0.001	Yes	Yes	Partial Mediation

	direct effect	**95% confidence intervalof direct effect**	**T-value**	**Sig. p<0.05?**	**Indirect effect**	**95% confidence interval effect**	**T-value**	**P – value**	**Indirect effect Sig.**	**Direct effect Sig.**	**Conclusion**
Thr->Mgt_d->Unxch->DE	0.315	(0.143-0.501)	3.423	0.000	0.081	(0.017-0.183)	1.780	0.076	No	Yes	Full Mediation
Thr->DE->R_M_P	0.861	(0.791-0.919)	26.278	0.000	0.271	(0.122-0.420)	3.415	0.001	Yes	Yes	Partial Mediation
Thr->Mgt_d->Unxch->DE->R_M_P	0.237	(0.076-0.443)	2.529	0.012	0.070	(0.014-0.158	1.771	0.077	No	Yes	Full Mediation
Thr->Mgt_d->Unxch->DE->Org_Act	0.146	(0.070-0.215)	4.038	0.000	0.012	(0.002-0.028)	1.668	0.097	Yes	No	Full Mediation
Thr->DE->Org_Act	0.146	(0.070-0.215)	4.038	0.000	0.046	(0.018-0.096)	2.510	0.012	Yes	Yes	Partial Mediation
Thr->DE->R_M_P->Org_Act	0.852	(0.777-0.914)	25.206	0.000	0.231	(0.104-0.374)	3.374	0.001	Yes	Yes	Partial Mediation

	direct effect	95% confidence intervalof direct effect	T-value	Sig. p<0.05?	Indirect effect	95% confidence interval effect	T-value	P – value	Indirect effect Sig.	Direct effect Sig.	Conclusion
Thr->Mgt_d->Unxch->DE->R_M_P->Org_Act	0.852	(0.777-0.914)	25.206	0.000	0.012	(0.003-0.031)	1.664	0.097	Yes	No	Full Mediation
Vul->Mgt_d->Unxch	0.596	(0.417-0.828)	5.864	0.000	0.553	(0.388-0.759)	5.997	0.000	Yes	Yes	Partial Mediation
Vul->Mgt_d->Unxch->DE	0.928	(0.885-0.912)	56.420	0.000	0.313	(0.045-0.235)	2.495	0.013	Yes	Yes	Partial Mediation
Vul->DE->R_M_P	0.437	(0.241-0.626)	4.588	0.000	0.376	(0.210-0.552)	4.423	0.000	Yes	Yes	Partial Mediation
Vul->Mgt_d->Unxch->DE->Org_Act	0.146	(0.077-0.205)	4.377	0.000	0.019	(0.006-0.042)	2.249	0.025	Yes	Yes	Partial Mediation

	direct effect	**95% confidence intervalof direct effect**	**T-value**	**Sig. p<0.05?**	**Indirect effect**	**95% confidence interval effect**	**T-value**	**P – value**	**Indirect effect Sig.**	**Direct effect Sig.**	**Conclusion**
Vul->Mgt_d->Unxch->DE->R_M_P->Org_Act	0.237	(0.071-0.434)	2.616	0.009	0.096	(0.030-0.187)	2.394	0.017	Yes	Yes	Partial Mediation
Vul->DE->Org_Act	0.437	(0.241-0.626)	4.588	0.000	0.064	(0.028-0.106)	3.151	0.002	Yes	Yes	Partial Mediation
Vul->DE->R_M_P->Org_Act	0.852	(0.795-0.915)	27.555	0.000	0.320	(0.179-0.472)	4.385	0.000	Yes	Yes	Partial Mediation
Vul->Mgt_d->Unxch->DE->R_M_P->Org_Act	0.852	(0.795-0.915)	27.555	0.000	0.096	(0.030-0.187)	2.394	0.017	Yes	Yes	Partial Mediation
Mgt_d->Unxch->DE	0.928	(0.886-0.955)	55.946	0.000	0.220	(0.064-0.392)	2.591	0.010	Yes	Yes	Partial Mediation

	direct effect	95% confidence intervalof direct effect	T-value	Sig. p<0.05?	Indirect effect	95% confidence interval effect	T-value	P –value	Indirect effect Sig.	Direct effect Sig.	Conclusion
Mgt_d->Unxch->DE->R_M_P	0.237	(0.071-0.434)	2.616	0.009	0.189	(0.048-0.288)	2.573	0.010	Yes	Yes	Partial Mediation
Mgt_d->Unxch->DE->Org_Act	0.237	(0.071-0.434)	2.616	0.009	0.032	(0.011-0.068)	2.284	0.025	Yes	Yes	Partial Mediation
Mgt_d->Unxch->DE->R_M_P->Org_Chr	0.852	(0.795-0.915)	27.555	0.000	0.161	(0.048-0.288)	2.542	0.011	Yes	Yes	Partial Mediation
Unxch->DE->R_M_P	0.237	(0.071-0.434)	2.616	0.009	0.204	(0.061-0.359)	2.604	0.010	Yes	Yes	Partial Mediation
Unxch->DE->Org_Act	0.146	(0.077-0.205)	4.377	0.000	0.035	(0.012-0.071)	2.307	0.021	Yes	Yes	Partial Mediation

	direct effect	95% confidence intervalof direct effect	T-value	Sig. p<0.05?	Indirect effect	95% confidence interval effect	T-value	P – value	Indirect effect Sig.	Direct effect Sig.	Conclusion
Unxch->DE->R_M_P->Org_Act	0.852	(0.773-0.914)	27.555	0.000	0.174	(0.052-0.307)	2.571	0.010	Yes	Yes	Partial Mediation
DE->R_M_P->Org_Act	0.852	(0.773-0.914)	27.555	0.000	0.733	(0.658-0.799)	20.205	0.000	Yes	Yes	Partial Mediation

The indirect effects were defined as the sequence of relationships that involved at least one intervening construct, as shown in the diagram. Here, the indirect effect p1.p2 represents the mediating effect of the risk management practice construct (R_M_P) on the relationship between SoE attack risk (Vul, Thr, Mgt_d, Unxch, DE) and Organizational Characteristics (Org_Act). From the observation, it was shown that Thr->Mgt_d->Unxch->DE >Mgt_d->Unxch->DE->R_M_P-> Org_Act were fully mediated. This means that the independent variable Organizational Activities (Org_Act) did not have a significant effect on the dependent variables after the inclusion of the mediation variables. However, another effect showed that it had partial mediation. The independent variable Organizational Activities (Org_Act) has a significant effect on the dependent variables after the inclusion of the mediation variables.

4.5. Moderator variable for the Model

The moderator variable could change the strength of the relationship between the exogenous and endogenous latent variables.

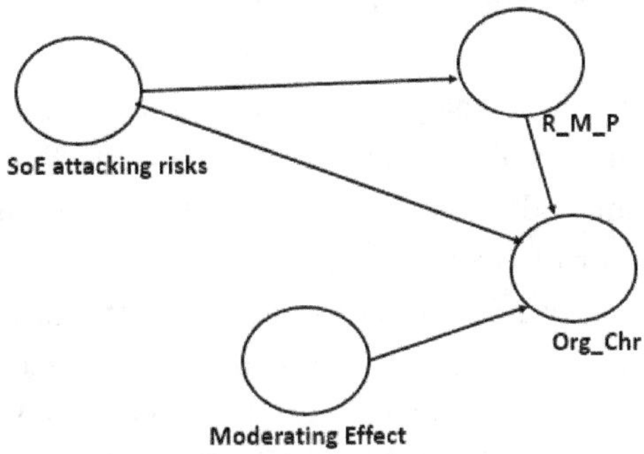

Figure 4.3: Moderating effect of the research model

Table 4.18: Moderating effect values

	Original Sample(O)	**Sample Mean(M)**	**2.5%**	**97.5%**
DE->Org_Act	0.150	0.148	0.083	0.215
DE->R_M_P	0.861	0.860	0.797	0.915
Mgt_d->Unxch	0.928	0.931	0.897	0.958
Moderating Effect >Org_Act	0.008	0.007	0.019	0.024
R_M_P >Org_Act	0.857	0.858	0.796	0.913
Thr->DE	0.315	0.316	0.142	0.483
Thr->Mgt_d	0.368	0.364	0.149	0.550
Unxch->DE	0.237	0.241	0.077	0.425
Vul->DE	0.437	0.432	0.234	0.625
Vul->Mgt_d	0.596	0.601	0.421	0.802

The moderating effect provides evidence that, risk management is necessary for preventing SoE attacks in organizations. An exploratory analysis digs deeper into the risk management practices for preventing SoE attacks in organizations. A quantitative approach was used to explore these issues, as this method allows the inner experience of the participants to be captured, to determine how meanings are formed, rather than merely through testing variables. The method is often used when the researcher is interested in obtaining detailed and rich knowledge on specific phenomena, particularly in an area where the researcher has little information or knowledge of the research problem. Perhaps, an exploratory design is highly useful for discovering new relationships, patterns, themes and ideas in research problems. An exploratory analysis examined risk management practices for preventing SoE attacks in Malaysian organizations through a qualitative content analysis method. The same method was successfully employed by other researchers for discovering and creating new knowledge in the field. This approach is defined as a research technique for making replicable and valid inferences from texts to the context of their use. Content analysis was selected to help meet the fourth objective of the study, for example, to develop an information security framework for preventing SoE attacks. This exploratory study also assessed how organizations manage SoE attack risk in the organization, an in- semi structured method was used to distribute the questionnaire and further investigate the empirical results. The exploratory analysis is described in greater detail in the subsequent section. The exploratory analysis employed a qualitative research approach and focused on semi structured methods. Semi structured methods were used in eight (8) organizations. Three steps were involved in this technique. The step involved reading all the transcripts several times to gain understanding of the data and its actual meaning so that similarities and differences could be identified. The second step involved an in-depth semi structured method involving the use of a distributed questionnaire, which enabled the researcher to identify similarities and differences. The content analysis was conducted manually throughout the process of identifying, coding and categorizing responses. The text representing the different categories and themes was highlighted and tabulated so that these were unambiguous and clearly defined. The final step involved refining and finalizing the theme. This was done by grouping relevant concepts. These categories and sub categories were subsequently rechecked.

Figure 4.4 illustrates the steps applied in this study.

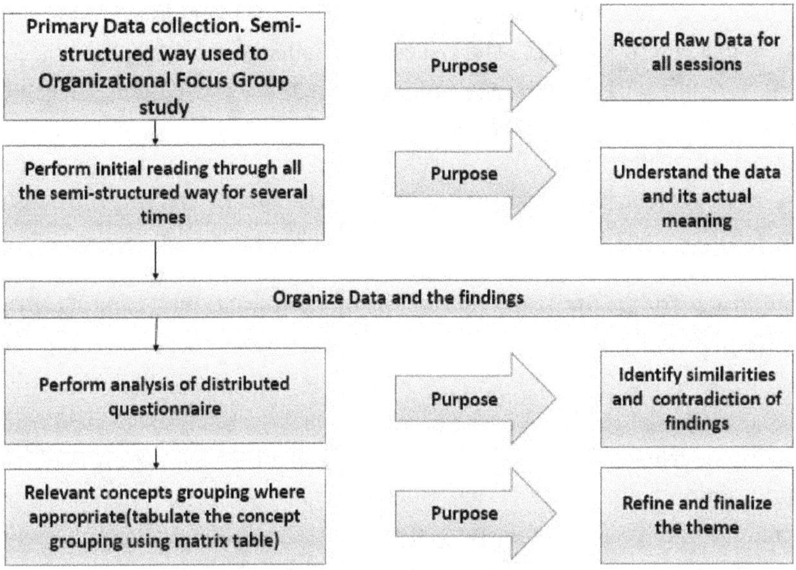

Figure 4.4: Exploratory Study Activities

To obtain deeper insights into SoE attack risk management practices in organizations. A semi structured method was used to distribute the questionnaires to eight organizations. The organizations involved in this semi structured process included various organizations, such as education sectors, the health care sector, banking and government agencies. The managers as and administrative employees were involved in these semi structured procedures; their ages ranged from 28 to 55 years, and they were experienced in awareness of the risks of SoE attacks in the organization. To avoid bias and to protect anonymity, these organizations are referred to as organizations A, B, C, D, E, F, G, and H. The focus group semi structured approach was used in various organizations by distributed relevant questionnaires. The purpose of the semi structured approach was to explore in- depth the management and operational practices for the prevention of risk from SoE attacks in organizations. Eight (8) focus groups of SoE attack risk awareness experts were semi structured to explore issues arising from the empirical study conducted earlier. The semi structured sessions were performed via a distributed relevant questionnaire on four (4) main risk management practices for the prevention of SoE attacks in the organization. Further investigation also highlighted the organizational practices of SoE attack risk studies before the implementation of the actual risk management practices for preventing SoE attacks. The exploratory analysis covered four (4) phases of SoE attack risk management practices. The issues and challenges of each phase faced by these organizations were analyzed as input for developing the initial framework (prevention technique of SoE attacks). Furthermore, the exploratory content analysis results regarding the organization's preliminary risk management practices for preventing SoE attacks were also discussed. The detailed analysis is reported in the next section.

Semi structured methods were used to investigate key practices during the SoE attack risk identification phase. Five organizations thoroughly practiced identifying the SoE attacks on digital evidence. Moreover, the other three organizations (A, B and C) partially practiced the identification phase of SoE attacks of digital evidence in the organizations. The analysis showed that all the organizations identified the SoE attack risks of digital evidence. Organizations A, B, C, D and E thoroughly identified the prevention technique of SoE attacks for saving their digital evidence, while organizations F, G and H were inconsistent in their practice of this. The inconsistency of these practices was attributed to human resources and time limitations. Another key activity was preparing proposals for SARM to the organization. Only three originations (B, G and H) claimed that they thoroughly practice this key activity. Managers and SoE attack risk awareness experts from organizations (A, F and G) said that they did not perform such activities about prepared proposals for SARM. Unfortunately, the other two organizations (C and D) did not conduct this activity at all. Managers and Senior Managers of the SoE attack risk awareness experts at organizations A, C, G, H and I partially practiced identification of related key components to the organizational evaluation of SARM proposal activities during the implementation of the prevention techniques for SoE attacks. The other organizations practiced this key activity since some of the key infrastructures were equipped with intelligent capabilities that made it difficult to manage the risk of the SoE attacking. In a semi structured way, most of the organizations claimed that they practice the identify the current security policies, standards and procedures for implementation. This was most important because some SoE attack risks can be prevented through appropriate security policies and the implementation of good information security management practices and procedures. Organizations A, B, C, D, E and F claimed that they do not have activity toward senior manager designate employees for risk management practice. They believed that this approach enabled senior management to gain a clear understanding of SoE attack risks in the organization. This proposal also minimizes the risk of SoE attack in organizations.

Finally, only organizations A, D and E reported that the SoE attack risk awareness practice was conducted. Despite having prepared for the necessary training, the other organizations did not directly report the completed SoE attack risk awareness to their outsider attackers. However, risk profiles were used among managers and SoE attack risk awareness experts in managing and mitigating SoE attack risks in organizations. Table 4.20 summarizes the results of the content analysis extracted from the semi structured method. The focus group was on activities conducted during the SoE attack risk identification phase. Three categories were used as indicators to classify risk management practices for the prevention of SoE attacks: 'Yes' for the activities/ tasks conducted; 'Partial,' for the activities / tasks partially conducted; and 'No,' for the nonconductors of activities/ tasks.

Table 4.19: Content analysis for the social engineering attack risk identification phase

Social engineering attacking risk identification phase: For the riskmanagement practice for the prevention technique of SoE attacks in the organizations	semi structured way was used of focus groups by distributed relevant questionnaire							
	A	B	C	D	E	F	G	H
1. Identify preliminary study for SoE attacking risk.	Partial	Partial	Partial	Yes	Yes	Yes	Yes	Yes
2. Preparing proposal of list of SoE attacking risks.	No	Yes	No	No	No	No	Yes	Yes

	A	B	C	D	E	F	G	H
3. Senior Management Evaluating the Proposal of the list of SoE attacking risk.	Partial	Yes	Partial	Yes	Yes	Partial	Partial	Partial
4. Senior Management designate organization's staffto responsible for the entire stages ofSoE attacking risks study, work together with SoE attacking risk awareness team members.	No	No	No	Yes	No	No	Partial	No
5. Defining SoE attacks and its awareness to each team member rolesand responsibilitiesfor the entire process of study.	Yes	Partial	Partial	Yes	Yes	Partial	Partial	Partial
6. Conducting a necessary training or work shop to theawareness of SoE attacking risks to the team on the process or procedure involved implementing the framework.	Yes	Partial	Partial	Partial	Yes	Yes	Partial	Partial

	A	B	C	D	E	F	G	H
7. Setting scope ofevaluation for SoE attacking risk management Studyfor the prevention technique of SoE attacks (Evaluationscope for digital evidence).	No	Partial	Partial	Partial	Partial	No	Partial	No
8. Describing and defining SoE attacking risk evaluation (human,process, technological risk related in the organization).	No	No	Yes	No	No	No	Yes	Partial
9. Describing and defining scope of SoE attacking riskssuch as (threats, vulnerability, management defects, unexpected change and digital evidence).	Partial	Partial	Partial	Partial	Partial	Yes	Yes	Partial
10. Describing anddefining scope of SoE attacking risks treatment, protection strategy, mitigation plan and activities plan to manage the prevention technique of SoE attacking risk.	Partial	Yes	Yes	Partial	Partial	Partial	Yes	Partial

Identification of SoE attack risk begins with identifying how organizational digital evidence is protected from SoE attacks. Semi structured methods were used by most of the organizations that conducted this activity. It was found that all the respondents identified the risk of the SoE attacking their organization. These SoE attack risks were classified into three categories (technology, human, process). The majority of the respondents identified digital evidence security requirements during this phase, producing a narrative description of the potential impact of SoE attack risks on the organization. Another group was sometimes unable to produce these narrative descriptions due to constraints in terms of the expertise and criticalness of the organizations, while some organizations did not produce the descriptions altogether. Moreover, the process of identifying key infrastructure components related to the organizational digital evidence, such as software, hardware, networking or communication media, was conducted by all respondents. The majority of the respondents identified current security policies, practices and procedures for their organizations, whereas some of the respondents prepared SoE attack risk profiles for organizational while most of them did not do so. The remaining prepared SoE attack risk profiles were only available when needed. At the end of this phase, the SoE attack risk profiles need to be reported to experts. The exploratory analysis concluded that most of the organizations practiced these key activities. As such, these key activities are recommended during the SoE attack risk identification phase. Additionally, participation from internal and external service provider staff was found to be crucial for reducing miscommunication among team members involved in organizational activities.

Semi structured methods were used to investigate the risk analysis phase preventing SoE attacks. The semi structured approach revealed the key activities conducted during this phase. The key activities identified from the exploratory study were as follows:

-Reviewing Organizational daily activity. Preparing a proposal of a list of SoE attack risks.

-Discussing and identifying SoE attacking risks attack risk issues or areas of concern.

-Creating awareness practices regarding SoE attacks.

-Defining SoE attacks and their awareness of each team member's roles and responsibilities for the entire process of study.

-Creating a vulnerability profile for digital evidence.

-Creating a threat profile for digital evidence.
-Creating a management defect profile for digital evidence.
-Creating an unexpected change profile for digital evidence.
-Creating an SoE attack risk from a digital evidence profile.
-Compelling and consolidating digital evidence, and security requirements to produce SoE attack risk descriptions. Organizations A, C and H reviewed the value of SoE attacks on digital evidence and thoroughly identified digital evidence related to organizational activities. Organization A partially conducted this activity, while two organizations (C and H) also conducted it altogether. Despite this, the two organizations also agreed that reviewing the value of SoE attacking risks on digital evidence was vital during the analysis of SoE attacking risks. Organization B claimed that they did not prepare any reviews for the prevention technique of SoE attacks or the current value for organizational impact despite the identification of the organizational impact. Conversely, organizations D, E, F and G did not establish the current value for organizational impact. This approach was deemed crucial for risk treatment planning to mitigate associated risks. No organizations partially conducted this key activity due to several constraints on expertise, human resources and time. The analysis revealed that establishing the current value in measuring the probability of an SoE attacking risk was conducted by organizations C, D and E. Organizations F and G partially conducted this key activity, while organizations A, B and H did not conduct this key activity during the SoE attack risk analysis phase. All the organizations were semi structured in prioritizing the review of SoE attack risks based on the nature of the risk and the organization's general tolerance for the risk during the SoE attack risk analysis phase. Moreover, organizations D and E determined the mitigation approach to minimize the probability of the SoE attacking risk and impacting the organization. The semi structured approach revealed that organizations C, F, G and H only conducted this key activity only partially. Unfortunately, organizations A and B did not conduct this key activity during the SoE attack risk analysis phase. However, they claimed that the mitigation approach was conducted during risk mitigation planning. Another key activity during the SoE attack risk analysis phase was to discuss the SoE attack risk issues, with sufficient guidance to set and revise mitigation priorities. Organizations A, B, D, F, G and H did

partially conduct this key activity, while organization H only conducted it partially. Only organizations C and E conducted this key activity. Managers and information security experts from organization F stated that prioritization of risk mitigation should be conducted with full participation of all team members. A final key activity conducted during the SoE attack risk awareness phase was creating the SoE attack risk profile in the context of organizational needs. Organizations A, D and E conducted this activity almost entirely organizations B, C and D partially conducted this activity because of resource and time constraints. Table 4.21 summarizes the results of the content analysis extracted from the focus group in a semi structured way on activities conducted during the SoE attack risk analysis phase in the organization. Three categories were used to classify the practices of risk management of prevention techniques for SoE attacks in this exploratory study. Three categories were used to classify the practices of SoE attack risk management in the organization in this exploratory study. 'YES' for the activities/ tasks conducted; 'Partial,' for activities / tasks partially conducted; and 'No' for the no conducting of activities/ tasks.

Table 4.20: Content analysis for the social engineering attack risk analysis phase.

Social engineering attacking risk analysis phase: the risk managementpractice for the prevention techniqueof SoE attacks in the organizations	Semi structured way of focus groups by distributed relevantquestionnaire							
	A	B	C	D	E	F	G	H
1. Reviewing Organizational daily activity.	Yes	No	Yes	No	No	No	No	Yes
2. Discussing and Identify SoE attacking risks issuesor areas of concerns.	Partial	Partial	Yes	Partial	Yes	Partial	Partial	Partial

	A	B	C	D	E	F	G	H
3. Creating awarenesspractice regarding SoE attacks.	No	No	Yes	No	No	Partial	Partial	No
4. Creating Vulnerability Profile for digital evidence.	Yes	Yes	No	No	Yes	No	No	Yes
5. Creating Threat Profile for digital evidence.	No	No	No	Yes	No	Partial	Partial	No
6. Creating management defects profile for digital evidence.	No	Partial	Yes	No	Yes	No	No	No
7. Creating unexpected change profile for digital evidence.	Partial	No	No	No	Yes	No	Partial	No
8. Creating SoE attacking risk of digital evidence profile.	Partial	No	No	No	Yes	No	Partial	No
9. Compelling and consolidating digital evidence, security requirement, to produce SoE attacking risks description.	Yes	No	No	No	Yes	No	Yes	No

The exploratory analysis concluded that most of the organizations practiced the nine (9) Key activities during the SoE attack risk analysis phase. Therefore, these nine (9) key activities are recommended during this phase.

The analysis results and highlights the importance of identifying SoE attack risks, such as the risk of SoE attack threats, the risk of SoE attack vulnerabilities, the risk of SoE attack management defects, the risk of SoE attack unexpected changes in management and the risk of SoE attack digital evidence. The association between risk management practices for preventing SoE attacks and organizational activities. In this research model, an advanced technique was usedto access a complex higher-order model that has many relationships. Confirmatory factor analysis was performed, and both unobserved and observed variables were incorporated. Furthermore, the study measured each item and explained the variance by multiple regression. Drawing upon these findings, it was important that information security experts in organizations pay urgent attention to minimizing the risk of SoE attacks in organizations. In terms of strategy, risk management practices for preventing SoE attacks should be managed. An exploration of the associations between various SoE attack risks revealed that SoE attack risks and risk management practices for preventing SoE attacks were associated with organizational activities. The investigated the relationship between interest at the second -order level. Further investigation of the characteristics of both factor analysis and multiple regression helps researchers simultaneously examine both direct and indirect effects of independent and dependent variables. However, SoE attacks risks and prevention technique in a digital evidence -based solution model enabled us to investigate the indirect incorporation of unobserved variable measures by indicator variables. These methods also facilitate accounting for measurement errors in unobserved variables. The results highlight the need for Malaysian organizations to focus more on preventing SoE attacks. However, the organizational strategy for the risk management practices also identifies the impact and minimization of SoE attack risks in various organizations. The model focused on the prediction of a specific set of hypothesized, relationships between SoE attack risk and risk management practices and maximized the explained variance in the dependent variables. Moreover, the structural model displayed the relationship (path) between the constructs. The measurement model displayed the relationship between the constructs and indicator variables.

In addition, the chapter highlights and analyses the measurement latent variables by reflective and formative measurements. Hence, the objective of this research was to investigate the structural model and explain the target constructs. However, the estimated coefficients of the path model relationship maximize the R square values for the target endogenous constructs. However, the formative measurement indicators of this research model were assumed to be error free. However, the reflective measurements of this research model included error terms associated with each indicator, which was not the case for formative measurements. However, the indicators of these research model models were highly strongly correlated. The measurement error was considered at the item level, which was similar to what was the case in factor analysis. The indicators associated with the construct were strongly correlated with each other. However, the reliability and validity of the reflective measurement model were ensured measures and therefore provides support for the use of the suability and other inclusion path models for SoE attacks and prevention techniques in digital evidence -based solutions. Given these similarities, these findings suggest that there were is enough evidence that the results of SoE attacks and prevention techniques in digital evidence -based solution models also exist in the population. Hence, the results were statistically significant. Research has shown that SoE attacks and risk management practices exist in various Malaysian organizations.

Fundamentally, the empirical findings suggest analyzing of the prevention technique of SoE attacks, which is vital for developing an information security framework for preventing SoE attacks. This was an exploratory study in which semi structured interviews were analyzed by various organizations to determine the impact of risk management practices on prevention techniques for SoE attacks. However, to analyze risk management practices for preventing SoE attacks in organizations, a distributed questionnaire was used for the focus group study. For security purposes, the organizational name would remain anonymous. This analysis was crucial for achieving the fourth objective of the study to develop an SoE attack risk management information security framework for the prevention technique of SoE attacks in the organization. Input obtained from multiple managers, employees and SoE attack risk awareness experts through a focus group in a semii- structured way enabled the exploration of the foundation of the framework. An exploratory study was also conducted to identify the key activities for each phase of SoE attack risk management that are appropriate for organizational activity. The semi- structured methods used were conducted with eight selected organizations and content analysis was conducted by using a distributed relevant questionnaire. Once the data were gathered, analyzed and tabulated for each, they were then compared and contrasted for a single analysis. In other words, a comparison of similar and diverse practices among the organizations was conducted. Overall, the organizations practiced almost all the phases of prevention techniques for SoE attack risk, such as SoE attack risk identification, SoE attack risk analysis, SoE attack risk treatment plan and SoE attack risk treatment plan implementation, and SoE attack risk monitoring and SoE attack risk control. However, there was divergence in the key activities practiced due to several factors, such as time constraints and the limited number of resources and experts. As a result, some organizations had to omit several key activities, such as providing guidance for weighting alternatives and allocating dedicated personnel to adjust the course of action plans and determining whether changing organizational conditions indicted the presence of new SoE attack risks. There is evidence to suggest that organizations are aware of this kind of SoE attack risk. However, there is no information security framework for preventing SoE attacks in the organizations. Therefore, implementing risk management for. preventing SoE attacks would minimize such attacks. An analysis of the risk management practices of the SoE as envisioned by managers and SoE experts in Malaysia revealed interesting results. Fundamentally, most of the organizations did not seriously consider how to manage the three risk factors for of SoE attacks. However, the organizations managed to establish plans to manage common SoE attack risks (SoE attack risk of threats, SoE attack risk of vulnerabilities, SoE attack risk of management defects in the organization, and SoE attack risk, risk of unexpected change in management, SoE attack risk of digital evidence), and this provides the basis for the development of an information security risk management framework for the prevention technique of SoE attacks in organizations. This study illustrated an emerging consensus on the importance of conducting preliminary work before implementing risk management for SoE attacks. It was also vital to obtain maximum support from top management to execute most key activities and provide sufficient information for preparing effective plans for managing SoE attack risks. Hence, it is recommended that some key activities during the preliminary work be conducted before the start of actual risk management processes involving SoE attacks. There is evidence that some organizations are conducting unique prevention techniques for SoE attack risk, with the main objective of minimizing the risk occurrence and impact on organizational business activities. However, since frameworks or standard guidelines limited and since not all the risk management steps associated with SoE attacks were adhered to and considered appropriate, a dedicated risk management framework for SoE attacks was proposed. The results of the exploratory analysis, therefore, suggest that it is crucial and timely to develop an SoE attack risk management framework that incorporates step-by-step guidelines that can assist SoE risk awareness, experts and information security experts in making strategic decisions to reduce SoE attack risks in organizations. This approach can help managers and information security professionals mitigate SoE attack risks to fully exploit the benefits to of continuing organizational activities. The following sections will present and discuss the development of an information security framework for preventing SoE attacks. In view of the weakness and difficulties of current organizational practices, organizations must adopt strategic approaches for managing and mitigating SoE attack risks.

Chapter Five

Fortifying the Fortress: Strategies for Risk ManagementFramework

5.1. Overview of Risk Management Framework

Social Engineering Attacking Risks are the major concern for organizations, particularly when implementing organizational activities. Despite the benefits of risk management practices for preventing SoE attacks, such practices provide protection from digital evidence. Thus, the viability of the strategy is dependent upon the security measures taken to minimize the risk of SoE attacks. In that case, if these SoE attack risks are not effectively and appropriately managed, then the full benefits of organizational activity will not be reaped and may also cause unforeseen repercussions for organizational functions and business activities. Therefore, organizations need to have proper guidelines or an appropriate framework to assist them in managing SoE attack risks for preventing such attacks. However, from the previous chapter discussion, it was found that risk management practices are necessary for preventing SoE attacks, and the framework is the finest way to manage SoE attack risks during organizational activity. The findings, as discussed in Chapter IV, revealed five emerging SoE attack risks in the organization. This leads to the full exploitation of risk management practices for prevention technique of SoE attacks that benefit the organization. Meanwhile, the findings suggest that some organizations omit important steps in managing these emerging risks. The exploratory study discussed in Chapter IV also showed that most of the organizations did not practice the measures focused on these five emerging SoE attack risks. Current available approaches to managing SoE attack risks should be tailored according to these five emerging risks for organizational activity implementation. Hence, a unique information security risk management framework for preventing SoE attacks in organizations is proposed. The framework will concentrate on the steps required to improve the process of risk management practice for the prevention technique of SoE attacks in the organization. The proposed framework provides structured and step-by-step guidelines and chronological linkages between processes and activities for the prevention of SoE attacks in organizations.

Various researchers have introduced their own methods to manage SoE attack risks. However, most of these studies are anecdotal and have empirical validation, especially because it is necessary to practice risk management practices to prevent SoE attacks during the implementation of organizational activities. Therefore, this study proposes a risk management framework for preventing SoE attacks in organizations. The framework takes into consideration previous literature for managing SoE attack risks. Thus, this approach is more reliable since it is also supported by theoretical perspectives and generic practices or managing such risks.

Additionally, Chapter V also discusses the issues and challenges of risk management practices for preventing SoE attack risks in organizations. The prevailing issues and challenges were analyzed and explored in view of the development of the proposed framework. The framework comprises a broad range of processes and activities (as shown in Figure 5.1), covering the entire spectrum of three stages (Stage 1: SoE attack risk of Preliminary Study, Stage II: SoE attack risk evaluation and planning; Stage III: SoE attack risk monitoring and control execution plan). As such, it is a specific tool for improving the efficacy of the entire SoE attack risk management process for the organization.

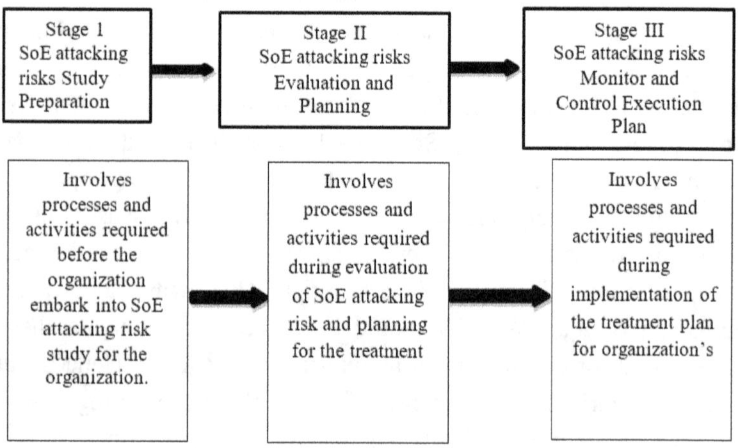

Figure 5.1: Stage of the Framework

Essentially, the framework for managing the risk of attack by SoE consists of these main stages. Each stage consists of several processes and activities. To highlight the contributions of this study, different notations were used to represent the processes and activities involved in the framework. The highlighted areas indicate the original contributions, while the dotted boxes indicate the partial contributions of the processes. Details about the framework components and contributions are discussed further later in the framework stage section. The framework components consist of several stages, processes and activities that, from its very understanding, involve the workings of each component. The framework overview is illustrated using text, highlighted or dotted lines and arrows. The highlighted representation indicates the original contribution, while the dotted representation indicates the partial contribution of the process. The components (activates) of the framework were tailored to suit the implementation of SoE attack risk management for the organization. Therefore, a combination of commonly used, optimized and totally new components is proposed to improve its implementation. Unique notations were used (as shown in Figure 5.2) to differentiate the components for the purpose of highlighting the contributions of the research. The three types of notations include the common component (represented by the solid line boxes), the Improvised Component (represented by dotted line boxes) and the proposed component (represented by solid bold line boxes).

No	**Notation Name**	**Graphical Representation of the component**	**Degree of Contribution**	**Description**
1	Common Component (Activity)		Common Practice (Improvised 20%-40% of common practice)	Apply current common practices of the approaches or processesor activities managing SoE attacking risk.

No	Notation Name	Graphical Representation of the component	Degree of Contribution	Description
2	Improvised Component (Activity)		Partial Contribution (Improvised 40%- 70% of Common Practices)	Improvise current common practices to apply in new environment, new application of activities,new factors involved, and application of common practices (process or activities) innew environment managing SoE attackingrisks.
3	New Proposed Component Activity		Solid contribution (Practice, Process, Perspective, Factor Subject area)	Proposed new practices (processes or activities) factors and approached,new focus perspective managing SoE attackingrisks. Shown in square shape.

Figure 5.2: Details of the notation used

The detailed components of these framework stages are illustrated in Figures 5.3, 5.4 and 5.5. The detailed elated processes and activities for each specific stage will be discussed in the next sections.

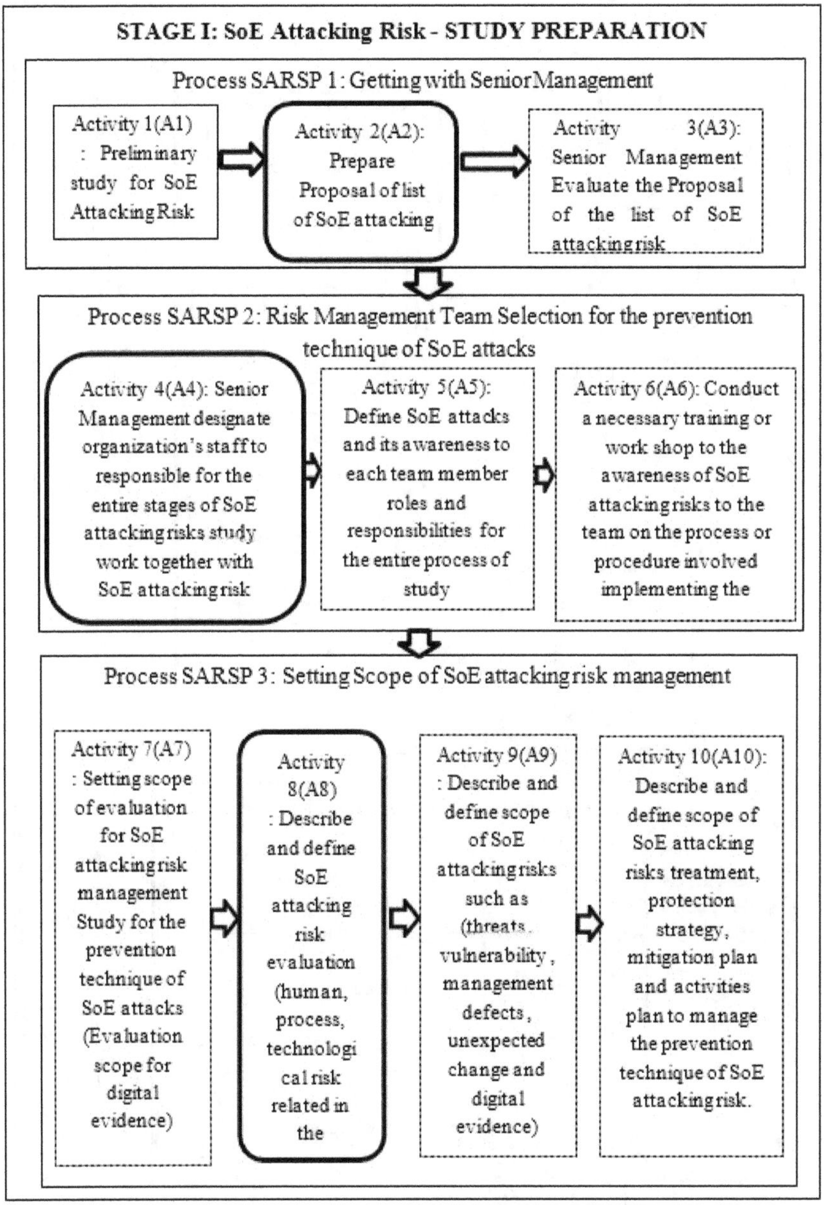

Figure 5.3: Stage I of the risk management framework for social engineering attacks and digitalprevention techniques

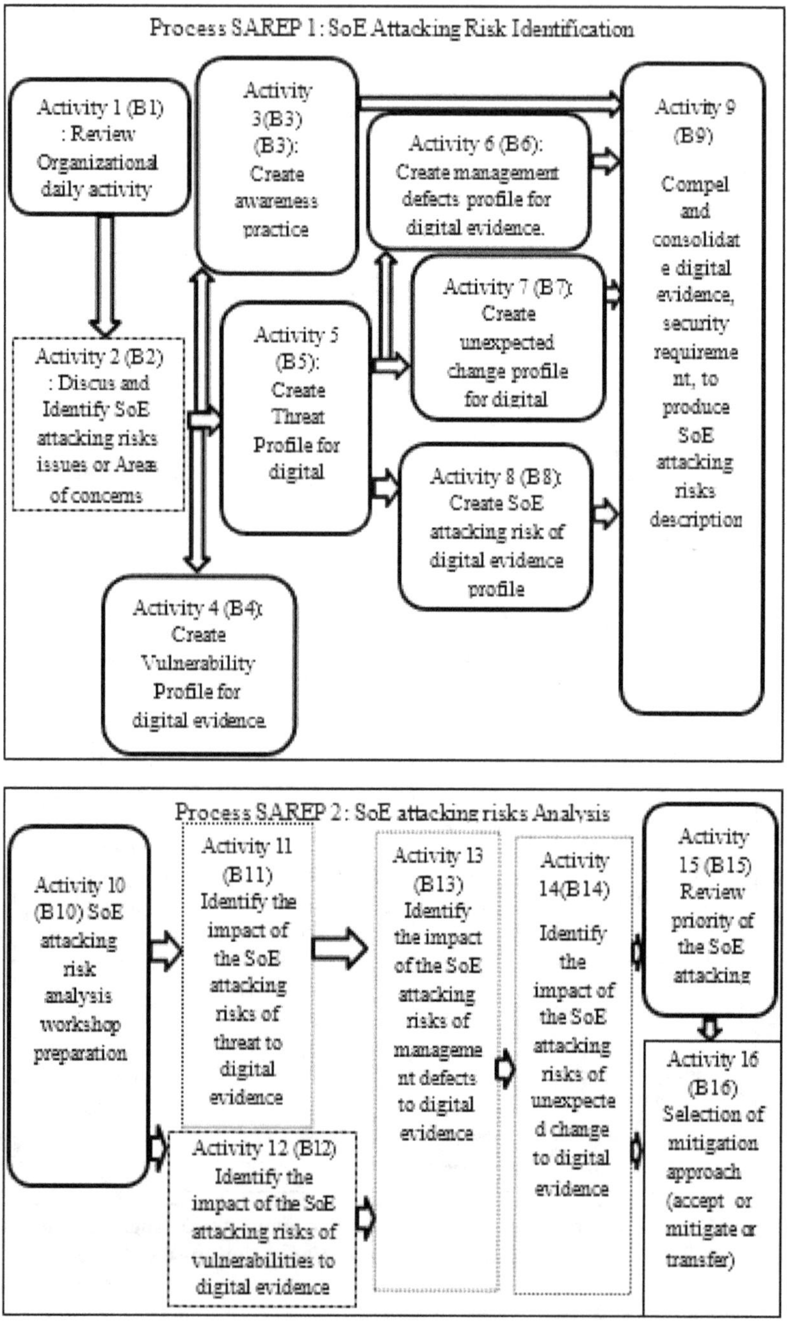
Process SAREP 1: SoE Attacking Risk Identification
Activity 1 (B1) : Review Organizational daily activity
Activity 3(B3) (B3): Create awareness practice
Activity 6 (B6): Create management defects profile for digital evidence.
Activity 9 (B9) Compel and consolidate digital evidence, security requirement, to produce SoE attacking risks description
Activity 7 (B7): Create unexpected change profile for digital
Activity 2 (B2) : Discus and Identify SoE attacking risks issues or Areas of concerns
Activity 5 (B5): Create Threat Profile for digital
Activity 8 (B8): Create SoE attacking risk of digital evidence profile
Activity 4 (B4): Create Vulnerability Profile for digital evidence
Process SAREP 2: SoE attacking risks Analysis
Activity 10 (B10) SoE attacking risk analysis workshop preparation
Activity 11 (B11) Identify the impact of the SoE attacking risks of threat to digital evidence
Activity 13 (B13) Identify the impact of the SoE attacking risks of management defects to digital evidence
Activity 14(B14) Identify the impact of the SoE attacking risks of unexpected change to digital evidence
Activity 15 (B15) Review priority of the SoE attacking
Activity 16 (B16) Selection of mitigation approach (accept or mitigate or transfer)
Activity 12 (B12) Identify the impact of the SoE attacking risks of vulnerabilities to digital evidence

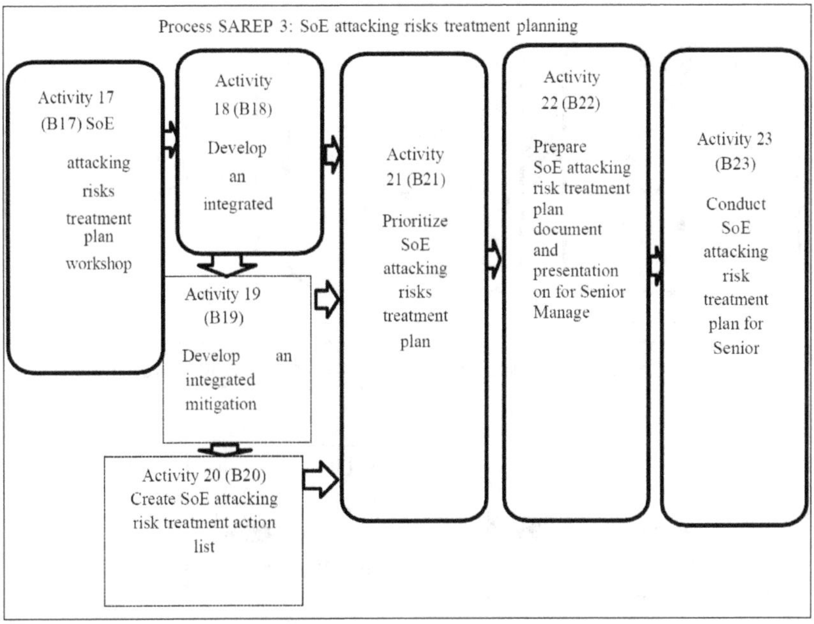

Therefore, the overall model would be:

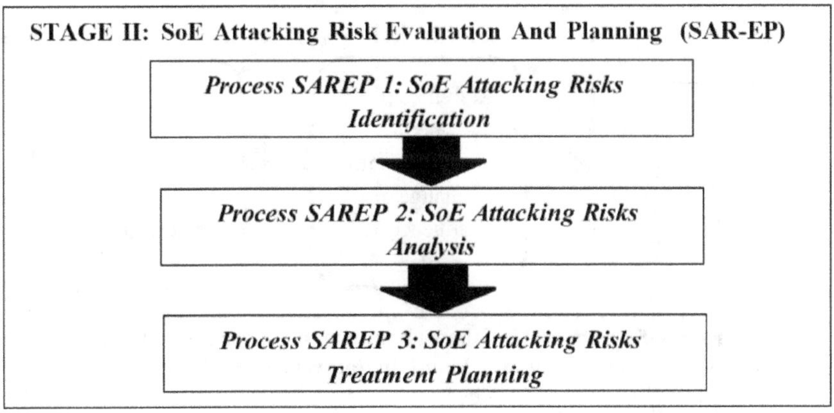

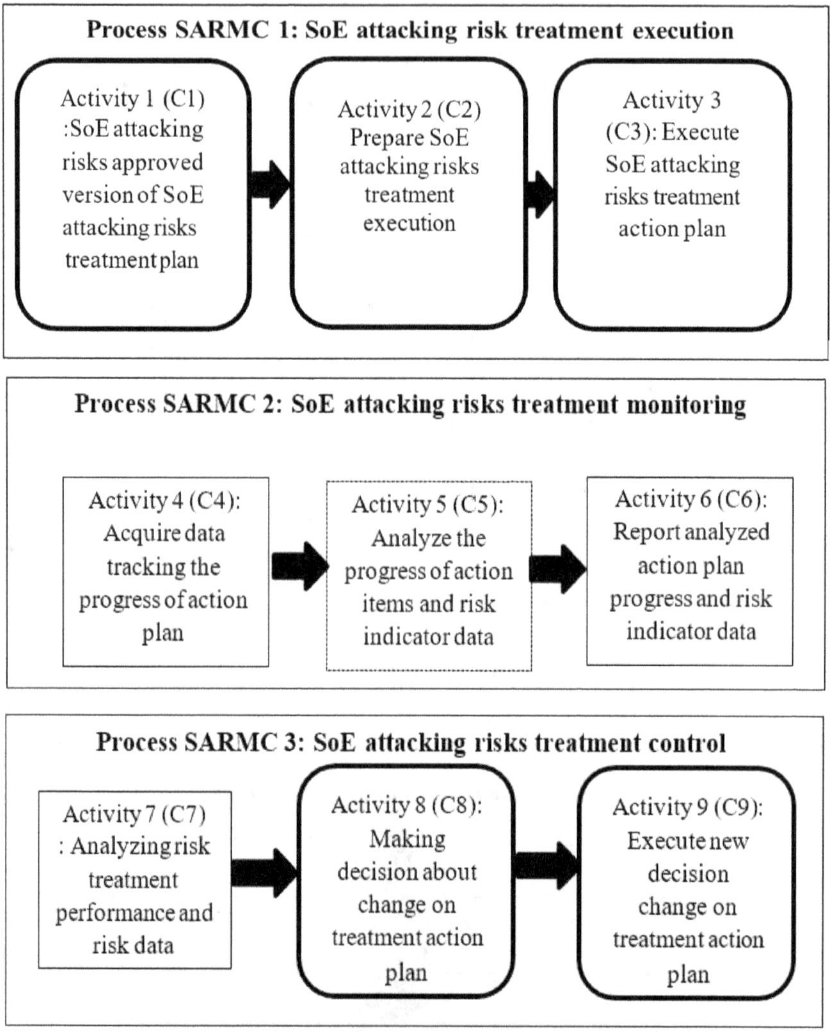

Figure 5.4: Stage III of the risk management framework for social engineering attack and digitalprevention techniques

Therefore, the overall process and activities are as follows:

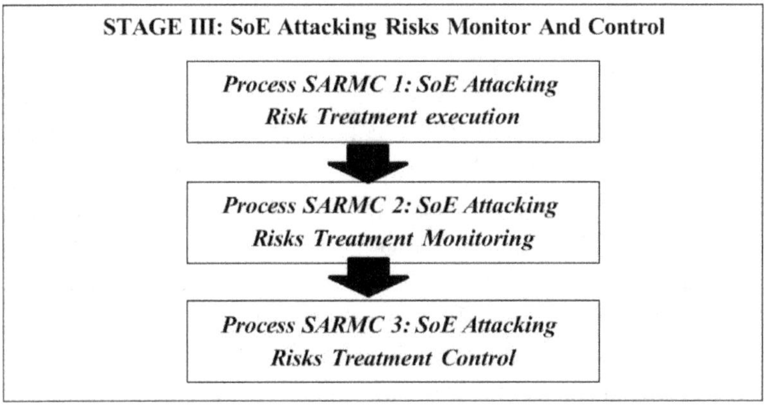

In each stage, the process and activity components of the framework on information security risk management for the prevention technique of SoE attacks describe its own high-level principles and objectives. The principles detail what needs to be done to meet the objective of each component.

5.2. The Framework Stages, Processes, Activities and Worksheets

The framework is divided into three different stages, each of which comprises several processes, and detailed activities; Figure 5.2 below shows the number of processes and activities involved in implementing the framework.

Table 5.1: Breakdown of the framework component according to stage

Stage	Number of Processes	Number of Activities
Stage I : SoE attacking risk studypreparation (SAR-SP)	3 Processes	10 Activities
Stage II : SoE attacking risk evaluationand planning (SAR-EP)	3 Processes	23 Activities
Stage III : SoE Attacking Risks Monitorand Control Execution plan (SAR-MC)	3 Processes	9 Activities
Total	**9 Processes**	**42 Activities**

Stage I of the framework consists of three major processes, namely, getting with senior management (SARSP1), team selection (SARSP2) and setting the scope of the SoE attack risk study (SARSP3). Each of these processes entails specific activities. Stage II of the framework also comprises three major processes, namely, SoE attack risk identification (SAREP1), SoE attack risk analysis (SAREP2) and SoE attack risk treatment planning (SAREP3). Each of these processes also involves the conduct of specific activities. Stage III consists of three interrelated processes conducted to monitor the risk and control the treatment execution. These processes include SoE attack risk treatment execution (SARMC1), SoE attack risk treatment monitoring (SARMC2) and SoE attack risk treatment control (SARMC3). Each of these processes comprises specific activities to be conducted. In addition to covering three distinct stages of managing SoE attack risk, the framework also includes additional materials (e.g., templates, worksheets, forms, and checklists) as easy and quick guides to organizations.

Accordingly, this part of the framework provides the following:

-Explanation of the three stages and summary table of each related process involved in the framework.

-Outline structure of the framework component.

The framework was uniquely designed to guide an appropriate and effective process and procedures for managing SoE attack risk in organizations. Details about each stage, process, activity and related form or template will be discussed further in the following section.

Several preparatory processes are required to ensure successful implementation of the entire process of management for the prevention technique of SoE attacks particularly in the organization. The three processes involve senior management in the organization, risk management team selection for the prevention technique of SoE attacks and setting the scope of risk management for SoE attacks. Stage I of the framework consists of three major processes, namely, getting with senior management (SARSP1), team selection (SARSP2) and setting the scope of the SoE attack risk study (SARSP3). Each of these processes entails specific activities. Stage II of the framework also comprises three major processes, namely, SoE attack risk identification (SAREP1), SoE attack risk analysis (SAREP2) and SoE attack risk treatment planning (SAREP3). Each of these processes also involves the conduct of specific activities. Stage III consists of three interrelated processes conducted to monitor the risk and control the treatment execution. These processes include SoE attack risk treatment execution (SARMC1), SoE attack risk treatment monitoring (SARMC2) and SoE attack risk treatment control (SARMC3). Each of these processes comprises specific activities to be conducted. In addition to covering three distinct stages of managing SoE attack risk, the framework also includes additional materials (e.g., templates, worksheets, forms, and checklists) as easy and quick guides to organizations.

Accordingly, this part of the framework provides the following:

-Explanation of the three stages and summary table of each related process involved in the framework.
-Outline structure of the framework component.

The framework was uniquely designed to guide an appropriate and effective process and procedures for managing SoE attack risk in organizations. Details about each stage, process, activity and related form or template will be discussed further in the following section. The three processes within Stage I are composed of a number of activities, each covering a specific task for the activities, each of which contains a set of descriptions required to conduct the activity. Each component comprises several specific activities as a guide for the organization to conduct the process. Table 5.3 below shows the number of processes, activities and worksheets involved in Stage I.

Table 5.2: Breakdown of the framework component (processes and activities in stage I)

Stage I SoE attacking risk study preparation (SAR- SP)	
Processes	Number ofActivities
Process SARSP1 Getting with senior management	3 Activities
Process SARSP2 SoE attacking risk management team selection	3 activities
Process SARSP 3 Setting scope for SoE attacking risk management	4 activities
Total	**10 Activities**

The overall component structure (processes and activities) and relevant worksheet outlines for this stage of the framework are illustrated in the following figures:

Figure 5.6 Stage I- Getting with Senior Management (Process SARP1). Figure 5.7 Stage I- SoE Attacking Risk Management Team Selection (Process SARP2). Figure 5.8 Stage I- Setting Scopefor SoE Attacking Risk Study (Process SARP3).

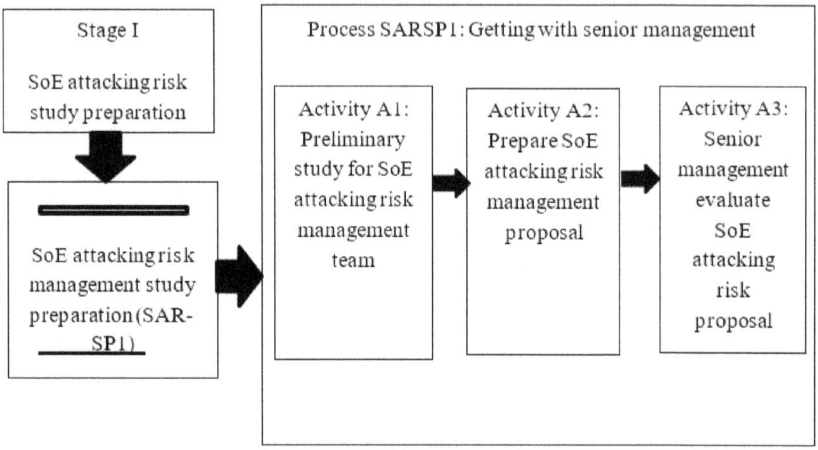

Figure 5.5: Structure of the framework component for Stage I (Process SARP1 –Getting with Senior Management)

5.3. Conduct necessary training or workshops

It is recommended that training or workshops be conducted to improve SARAT members' understanding of the processes and procedures to be implemented. Organizations could hire experts from outside to provide training or team members attached to any supplementary training available in the industry. The SoE attack risk evaluation and planning (Stage II) concentrate on evaluating the SoE attack risk, such as identifying and planning for the treatment of the risk. This is a critical stage, as identifying and analyzing the related SoE attack risk will contribute to the design of a suitable treatment plan. The three processes involved in evaluating and planning the risk of attack for SoE are risk identification, risk analysis, and risk treatment planning. Each of these processes entails specific activities. The three processes of Stage II comprise a number of activities, each of which contains a set of descriptions required to conduct the activity. Each component of the process comprises specific activities as a guide for the organizations. Table 5.6 below shows the number of processes and activities involved in Stage II.

Table 5.3: Breakdown of the Framework Component (Processes and Worksheet in Stage II)

Stage II SoE Attacking Risk Treatment Plan Evaluation and Planning (SAR-EP)		
Processes	**Number of Activities**	**Number of Worksheets**
Process SAREP1 SoE attacking riskidentification	9 Activities	2 Worksheet
Process SAREP2 SoE attacking risk analysis	7 Activities	1 Worksheet
Process SAREP3 SoE attacking risk treatmentplanning	7 Activities	1 Worksheet
Total	**23 Activities**	**4 Worksheet**

The SARAT team is responsible for review -related information to capture information for risk identification during the SoE attack. The main objective of these reviews is to collect relevant information on SoE attack risk issues or areas of concern, related digital evidence, the location of key component infrastructures, indications of threats and vulnerabilities, etc.

SARAT should review the following documents, but not be limited to:

- System and software user manual.
- Operation manual and procedure documents.
- System software requirement specification.
- System and software functional specification.
- Team profile (management and implementation).
- Service provider profile.
- Enterprise network design architecture.
- Database design architecture.
- SoE attacking risk incidents.
- Organizational digital evidence stored security policy.
- Service provider's digital evidence security policy.

It is recommended that a checklist of reviewed documents be prepared for the SoE attack risk identification worksheet to manage the number of documents to review. Please include additional document to be reviewed if any or remove documents which are not relevant. The SARAT team is responsible for conducting a brainstorming session to discuss and identify SoE attack risk issues and areas. A team is required to capture information on related information security issues, an organization's digital evidence, sources of threats and vulnerabilities and outcomes related to the organization's information security areas of concern. The SARAT team members are required to participate in the information security risk identification workshop (workshop 1). Brainstorming sessions will be conducted to discuss arising information security issues and identify related areas of SoE attack risk concerns. In the brainstorming session, the SARAT team is required to identify digital evidence and the rationale for the selection, source of potential threats, source of potential vulnerabilities and digital evidence. At the end of this activity (Activity B2), the team is required to prepare the organization for digital evidence as a potential source of threats, vulnerabilities and outcome scenario diagram. The worksheet (Appendix- VI) provides guidelines on what to discuss and what to identify for relevant activities in the SoE attack risk identification workshop (Process SAREP1). Please refer to these following sections for Activity B2:

- Section A – SoE Attacking Risk Issues.
- Section B – Digital Evidence and Rationale.
- Section C - Digital Evidence, Source of Potential Threats, Vulnerabilities and Outcomes.
- Section D – Organization Digital Evidence Potential Source of Threats, Vulnerabilities and Outcomes Scenario Diagram.

Initially, the descriptions, such as name, brief description, owner, user, service provider and duration, were recorded. Section A captures SoE attack risk issues and the severity of digital evidence. Section B describes the list of digital evidence and the rationale for why it is considered digital evidence. Moreover, Section C assists the SoE attack risk analysis team (SARAT) in identifying sources of threats, sources of vulnerabilities and outcomes related to digital evidence. Section D provides a graphical representation of the organization's digital evidence of potential sources of threats, vulnerabilities and outcomes. This section provides a snapshot of the SoE attack risk description scenarios for areas of concern to be identified and analyzed further.

SARAT is also responsible for creating a vulnerability profile for digital evidence. The team captured all the possibilities of treatment through the combination of reviewing related documents and brainstorming among team members. Generally, there are several questions to consider when creating the SoE attack risk of vulnerability profiles. There are (but not limited):

- What is the related digital evidence?
- How does the SoE attack risk of vulnerabilities occur? (Access Mode)
- Who determines the risk of the SoE attacking vulnerabilities? (Actor)
- SoE attack risk of vulnerability outcomes?
- SoE attack risk of vulnerability impact?

The team is required to create three groups of SoE attack risk vulnerability profiles, which are (1) vulnerability profiles for human factor problems, (2) vulnerability profiles for technology or system problems, and (3) vulnerability profiles for digital evidence. In creating the SoE attack risk of vulnerability profiles for human factor problems, SARAT is required to specifically identify the name of digital evidence, physical or logical access, actor, motive, outcome and impact in graphical notation diagrams. Normally, there are two possible types of actors involved in most cases of SoE attack at risk of vulnerability (internal or external), and the motive is accidental or deliberate. Consequently, outcomes of the motive could most likely include disclosure, modification, loss or destruction and interruption. Each of these outcomes likely has an impact on the entire organization. Then, the associated impact related to each category of outcomes is identified. The risk of creating SoE attacks on vulnerability profiles for technology and system problems and other problems were similar. The only difference is that the motive is not required to be specified. The SoE attack risk of vulnerability profiles should be created for, each piece of digital evidence involved. Every vulnerability profile for digital evidence created will be described in graphical notation. Please refer to Appendix VI – Section G for this exercise. Generally, the first box represents the name of the digital evidence, the second box represents how the risk of the SoE attacking vulnerabilities occurs through physical or logical access, the third box represents the internal or external actor responsible for the vulnerabilities, the fourth box represents the deliberate or accidental motive of the actor, and the fifth box represents the outcomes from the actor's action, such as disclosure modification, loss or destruction or interruption. The last box in the diagram represents the direct or indirect impact of the outcomes on the digital evidence. SARAT is required to define the organization's tolerance for risk by creating evaluation criteria. These criteria are measures against which to evaluate the type of impact described during the previous activity. An organization should explicitly prioritize known risks to mitigate all of them. Funding staff, and schedule constraints limit the number and extent to which risks can be addressed. The activity provides decision makers with additional information that they can use when establishing mitigation priorities. When conducting an activity, the SARAT should first review background information to define evaluation criteria that are suited to the organization. The following information should be reviewed:

- Strategic and operational plans that streamline with an organization's business objectives.
- Legal requirements, regulations, and standards of due care with the organization shouldcomply.
- Insurance information related to information security and information protection.
- Results from other risk management processes used by organizations.
- Impact description worksheet (result from previous activity).

The objective is to develop an understanding of any existing organizational risk limits based on strategic and operational plans, liabilities and insurance-related issues. These data are important in establishing evaluation criteria, as these criteria are highly contextual. In some cases, organizations will have risks that could result in loss of life, but others may not. Thus, it is crucial for organizations to define their own evaluation criteria by reviewing relevant background information.

The following questions are asked about each area of impact.

- What defines a "high" impact on the organization?
- What defines a "medium" impact on the organization?
- What defines a "low" impact on the organization?

SARAT seeks to define specific details that constitute high, medium and low risk for its organization. For example, when measuring productivity as an area of impact, a low impact on productivity might occur after three lost days, whereas a high impact might occur after three weeks. At the end of this process of SoE attack risk analysis, SARAT is required to review the entire analysis results and identify the most appropriate strategy for addressing the impacts identified earlier during the process of SoE attack risk analysis. To do this, the SARAT must select the right mitigation approach to minimize the impact severity and reduce the frequency of occurrence of SoE attacks. There are three common approaches used by organizations to determine the most appropriate approach for addressing the effects of the impact of an SoE attack, which include accepting, mitigating or transferring risks. The mitigation approach was influenced by the capacity of an organization to plan, implement and monitor all activities undertaken to address these impacts. After the risk treatment plan has been finalized, execution of the plan will take place. Monitoring and control processes are highly important for ensuring that the plan works as scheduled. In the SoE attack risk monitor and control execution plan, organizations are required to conduct three processes: SoE attack risk treatment execution, Information Security Risk Treatment Monitoring and SoE attack risk treatment control. Each of these has its own individual activities to be conducted accordingly. SoE attack risk treatment execution is the process of taking planned action to improve an organization's security posture. The objective of this process is to execute all action plans according to the schedule and success criteria that were defined during risk treatment planning, for SoE attacks. SoE attack risk monitoring is the process of tracking action plans to determine their current status and reviewing organization data for the purpose of identifying new risks or changes to existing SoE attack risks. The objectives of this process are to collect accurate, timely, and relevant information about the progress of action plans and any major changes to an organization's and service provider's operational environment that could indicate the existence of new SoE attack risks or significant changes to existing SoE attack risk. Treatment control is a process whereby designated personnel adjust the course of action plans and determine whether changing organizational conditions indicate the presence of new risks. The objective of this process is to make timely, informed and effective decisions about corrective measures for action plans and about whether to identify new SoE attack risks. The risk of SoE attack is one of the major risks in organizations. Therefore, an appropriate approach for managing this specific nature of risk is important. While many previous researchers have introduced risk management approaches and frameworks to manage SoE attack risk, none have focused on the specific approach of managing SoE attack risk in organizations. This gap provided the impetus for the development of the framework on SoE attack risk for the organization. Empirical and exploratory findings formed the basis for the framework development. The development of the framework will allow organizations to have structured, step-by-step processes and activities in managing SoE attack risk. The framework for information security risk management for preventing SoE attacks in organizations involves innovative processes and procedures used to manage the risk of such attacks. The framework addresses SoE attack risk from a business -to -technological perspective, providing practical and appropriate risk management approaches for managing SoE attack risk in the organization. This chapter provides a detailed explanation of the framework on information security risk management for prevention technique of SoE attacks in the organization. First, a brief introduction to the framework is provided, explaining what the framework consists of and highlighting the key benefits of using the framework. The framework consists of three stages.

Stage I: The SoE Attacking Risk Study Preparation, covers processes and activities relating to the SoE attacking risk study preparation for the organization. The processes conducted at this stage include (1) working with senior management, (2) performing risk management team selection, on SoE attacks, and (3) setting the scope of the risk management study on SoE attacks.

Stage II: The SoE attack risk evaluation and planning covers processes and activities related to the process of evaluating the SoE attack risk and treatment plan to mitigate the risks involved in the organization. The processes conducted at this stage are-

(1) The risk identification of SoE attacks, (2) the risk analysis, of SoE attacks, and (3) therisk treatment plan for SoE attacks.

Stage III: The SoE attack risk monitor and control execution plan, covers processes and activities relating to the execution, monitoring and control of the risk treatment plan. Processes conducted at this stage include (1) executing the SoE attack risk treatment plan, (2) monitoring theSoE attack risk, and (3) controlling the SoE attack risk. This chapter also provides a comprehensive template, worksheets of checklist used within the framework, and references for each componentof the framework to guide the implementation of the framework.

Fundamentally, the contribution of the framework is that it provides a structured guide. This includes the categorization of several stages of the SoE attack risk management approach, thedesign of appropriate processes and activities tailored to the organization, the introduction of additional processes and activities to cater to emerging SoE attack risk factors and the development of comprehensive stages, processes and steps activities. All these are further supplemented with related worksheets and documents to work on in a structured manner. The proposed framework can guide information security professionals, and information technology experts to identify, analyze, and plan for treatment, and monitor and control information security risks comprehensively within the organization. The framework is considered to be a knowledge contribution to how organizations manage SoE attack risk. This dedicated framework introduces an innovative approach for managing existing and emerging risk factors for SoE attacks when implementing organizational activities. The innovative approach improves current practices through several additional processes to cater to specific emerging risk factors for SoE in the organization. By tailoring the process of implementing SoE attacks to suit organizational activities, the process of managing SoE attack risk practices. can be improved. Moreover, adding new knowledge to existing processes for managing information security, specifically for implementing organizational activities, would be another contribution. By improving the existing process, the application of the proposed framework will directly contribute to formulating more effective information security management plans, particularly in most organizational activities. Thus, the introduction of this framework contributes to significant improvements in the current process and practices for managing SoE attack risk in the organization. Finally, the introduction of this framework indirectly increases information security confidence in preventing the risk of SoE attacks in organizations.

Chapter Six

Building a Culture of Security: Framework Confirmatory

6.1. Overview of Framework Verified

The proposed framework will be verified through an expert-judgment approach to verify its acceptability and applicability for the organization, practitioner and research community. Experts in the field of information security, and managers were identified for the confirmatory study. For the purpose of this study, subject-matter- experts (SMEs) were selected to verify and validate the stages, processes, activities, tasks and worksheets of the framework. Furthermore, the substantial feedback, recommendations and rationales obtained were analyzed to enhance the framework. This chapter explains how the expert judgment method was applied to verify and validate the proposed framework components. The discussion begins with how the method is applied to validate the framework applicability and suitability and the results of the findings. In particular, the generic phases of an expert judgment method and how the method was applied for the framework confirmatory study are discussed. Preliminary analysis results on the selection of the organization are needed for discussion. The expert judgment results enabled the researcher to draw conclusions on the applicability and suitability of the proposed framework in actual organizational environments. The expert judgment method was used to verify the acceptability and applicability of the proposed framework in organizations. To this finally, a generic step of conducting the expert judgment was adopted, and two kinds of actors were involved in the expert judgment method, the experts and the analyst. Experts are the people who possess the required knowledge, and the analyst is the individual who conducts the expert judgment exercise. For the framework validation, the confirmatory study considered experienced information security consultants, specialists and managers from industry as experts.

Moreover, the researcher was considered the analyst who conducted the expert judgment exercise and concluded the findings. Figure 7.1 illustrates the scope of the expert judgment used to verify and validate the SARM framework for the organization in this study.

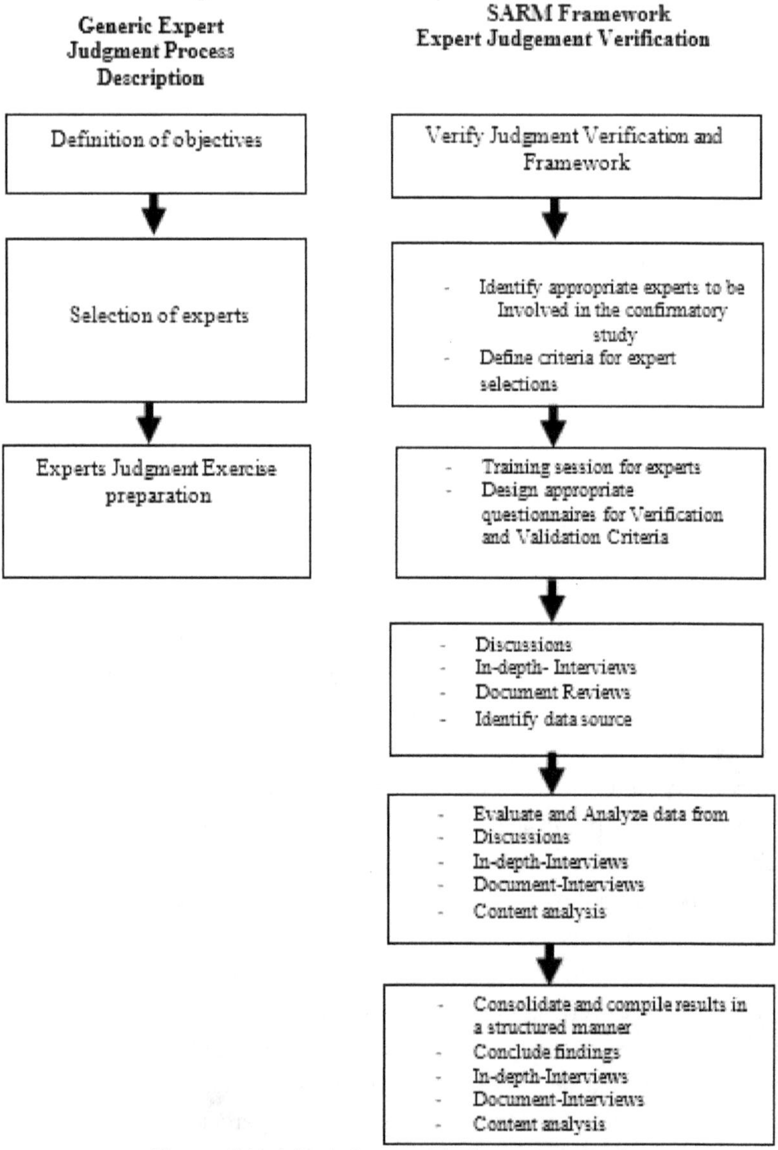

Figure 6.1: Adopted expert judgment method for the proposed framework validation

6.2. Results and discussion of the framework of the confirmatory study

Expert judgments can, and routinely are, employed in a host of varying manners, from roundtable discussions to more formalized forecast assessments such as the Delphi Method. Expert judgment requires the synthesis of expert opinions about a subject for whom there is uncertainty due to insufficient data or when such data are unavailable because of physical constraints or lack of resources. However, a generic expert judgment method tailored to the purpose of the study was adopted, as illustrated. Several criteria were used for the selection of experts who were responsible for evaluating and providing their judgment to validate the applicability and acceptability of the framework. The selected experts had sufficient domain knowledge, cognitive skills, decision strategies and expert task congruence related to SoE attack risk management in the organization. The selected experts had more than 15 years of extensive experience involved in organizational information security. All the experts had master's degrees. Additionally, one of the experts possesses the globally recognized Information Security Professional Certification (CISSP). To ensure reliable input of domain knowledge for framework confirmatory study, experts were selected from among senior positions and specialists as chief information security consultants or certificates. Professional or specialist. The cognitive skills of the experts about SoE attack risk management also contributed to the reliability of the framework's confirmatory judgments. Appropriate expertise in research discipline tasks allows experts to clearly understand the research subject and provide consistent judgment for framework validation. The main purpose of this confirmatory study was to assess the acceptability and applicability of the proposed framework for the organization. Therefore, the criteria for focus were whether the framework components are suitable for managing SoE attack risk and how the framework could be applied in the industry. Three documents were used when conducting the expert judgment method, namely, the framework user manual, worksheet, checklist and form and Expert Judgment Evaluation Worksheets. In general, the SMEs verify and validate the stages, processes and activities proposed in the Framework User Manual. Then, information from the Worksheet, Checklist and Form was collected as feedback for aggregation of the experts' replies. Preparation of the Expert Judgment Evaluation Worksheet Facilitated the process of collecting, combining and synthesizing the experts' opinions related to the objectives.

Preparing before discussions and evaluating the expert's responses to identified issues helped the researcher to have a clear understanding of the framework components and its capacity to manage information security risks for the prevention technique of SoE attacks in the organization.

Elicitation of expert opinion through a questionnaire was acknowledged to be more difficult than through a face-to-face, one-on-one interview. Moreover, by keeping the questions simple, the study attempted to avoid the pitfalls of potential misunderstanding. Patients were asked for self-assessment of those judgment where the expert felt less certain. For the purpose of this research, the Expert Judgment evaluation Worksheet was used as the primary evidence for verification and validation of the proposed framework. Experts were asked to review the components of the framework and evaluate the appropriateness of the SARM framework in the organization. The experts' rationales were also captured and documented. The results were subsequently used as an input for the aggregation of the findings. The expert judgment evaluation of the proposed framework was conducted for every stage. The expert judgment results from the Expert Judgment Evaluation Worksheet and other sources of findings were considered input for the aggregation of expert replies. The complete analysis documents the experts' judgment of the applicability and acceptability of the proposed framework. With years of experience in the organization, best practices for handling such activities have been established. However, those practices focused more on organizational risk management. Specifically, this approach is applied in SoE attack risk management to mitigate and tolerate failure risks in deliverables. As part of their information security efforts, additional aspects of information security management were suggested. These included the evaluation of the risk of the SoE attacking management defects and the risk of the SoE attacking unexpected changes due to service providers. The aggregations of the expert replies from the study were synthesized to further validate the findings.

Previous findings identified SoE attack risk as one of the most critical risks in the organization. Therefore, a dedicated framework must be established to address this issue. Before the framework components were proposed, a survey was conducted on 384 respondents from various organizations. Crucially, three additional SoE attack risk factors were discovered in addition to the SoE attack risk of threats and the SoE attack risk of vulnerabilities when dealing with organizational activities. The risk factors were the risk of managing defects being attacked by the SoE and the risk of unexpected changes being created by the service provider. Hence, the SoE attacks the risk of digital evidence when there are problems with the CIA triad in the organization. As a result, a framework for information security risk management for preventing SoE attacks was developed based on these findings. The framework addresses SoE attack risk from a business -to-technological perspective, providing practical and appropriate risk management approaches for managing information security in the organization.

Stage 1 of the framework involves the processes and activities required before the organization embarks on SoE attacking risk study for the organization. Therefore, the three processes in stage I were verified and validated by capturing the necessary data to assess the framework's acceptability. The following section describes the results and findings elicited from experts. The expert judgment on Stage I (SoE attack risk study preparation) and its components generally affirmed its high applicability and acceptability. The process of accessing senior management involved the preliminary SARM study, its proposal and senior management's review of the proposal. All the experts rated these steps as highly applicable and recommended that the preliminary study parameters be well defined and given sufficient allocation for risk management studies. Similarly, they stressed that the proposal had to be comprehensive and emphasize the benefits of the SARAT, while the evaluation must be performed by a specific committee who is aware of the evaluation criteria. The next component of stage I involves the SARM–SARAT team selection. The first step of team identification by senior management was rated as moderately applicable, as the experts warned that there may be a lack of available resources. The identification of SARAT roles was rated as highly applicable and useful because the experts remarked that clear role identification and understanding were imperatives. The provision of training for SARAT team members was, however, rated as moderately applicable and acceptable, with the experts affirming that this should be conducted when needed, depending on proper study. Finally, the component on setting the scope of the SoE attack risk study was rated as highly applicable and acceptable. The first step of setting the scope of evaluation for SoE attack risk studies was recommended as a key step in SAR studies, while the experts singled out the fourth step of describing and defining the scope of digital evidence protection strategies, mitigation plans and action plans as those that mustbe given ample time and resources. The experts also warned of the need to avoid inconsistencies in the action plan. It was also deemed necessary and common practice to conduct the second and third steps, which are to describe and define the scope of the SoE attack risk for the evaluation and to describe and define the scope of the responsible operational area.

Table 6.1: Key Summary of Expert Judgment Evaluation – Stage I

Stage I: SoE Attacking Risk Study Preparation				
Framework Components		**Applicability**	**Acceptability**	**Experts feedback**
SARSP 1 (Getting with Senior Management)	A1 (Preliminary Study for SARM)	High	High	Important identify scope
	A2 (Prepare SARM Proposal)	High	High	Proposal must be brief
	A3 (Senior Management Evaluate SARM Proposal)	High	High	Define evaluation criteria
SARSP 2 (SARM-SARAT Team Selection)	A4 (Senior Management Evaluate SARM-SARAT Proposal	Moderate	Moderate	Normally
	A5 (Define SARAT roles and Responsibilities for the entire process of study	Moderate	High	Clearly define the awareness of SoEattacks
	A6 (Conduct necessary training or workshop for SARAT team members)	Moderate	Moderate	Sometimes

Framework Components		Applicability	Acceptability	Experts feedback
SARSP 3 (Setting Scope of SoE Attacking Risk Study)	A7 (Setting Scope of Evaluation for SoE Attacking Risk Study)	Moderate	Moderate	Relate SoE to technological issues
	A8 (Describe and define SoE Attacking Risk scope for the evaluation)	high	Moderate	SoE attacking risk must be define clearly
	A9 (Describe and define the scope of SoE attacking risk)	Moderate	Moderate	Common practices
	A10 (Describe and define scope of SoE attacking risk treatment)	Moderate	Moderate	Applicable but a lot of time and resource needed

The captured data on the preliminary study of risk management for SoE attacks and relatedinput for proposal preparation. The experts strongly agreed that senior management was the key element in ensuring the success ofSARM in the organization. Specifically, the data captured showthat identifying the preliminary impact is also necessary. For example, the availability of a Data Recovery Centre (DRC) is one of the SoE attack risks of digital evidence issues. The potential impact normally involves data or information related to the system. The potential impact includessuch data or information itself services, business processes and the organization's reputation. A brief description ofthe SoE attack risk management plan was clearly provided in the proposal. The experts strongly suggested that, senior management should provide support through finance, human resources, technology and policy support in implementing SARM for the organization. Theresults show that there are similarities in the activities accepted by the organization during the process of getting with senior management. However, the data collection tools used differed slightly. The framework suggested that two group members to participate in the SARM study. These two team members are individuals from the organization and service provider. Theestablishment of a worksheet could capture team member details for SARAT. The selection of a team member should occur inside the organization, and the team member should have minimum skills, be aware of the risk of SoE attack and be familiar with the technologies related to the organization. Based on the feedback from experts, similar activities were conducted even though they were not specifically split into the SARAT.

6.3. Expert Judgment Results: Setting the Scope of the SoE attack risks:

Experts verified that the application of this process, as well as well-defined scopes facilitated the management and delivery. The expert judgment verified the importance of information security professionals being able to link the protection strategy, mitigation plan and action plan list with SoE attack risk. The scope of the protection strategy focuses on how the organization sets up a strategy to safeguard digital evidence for the organization. The scope of the mitigation plan explains how the organization plans to reduce the impact of the risk of SoE attacks. Action lists with detailed activities that describe the mitigation plan. For this purpose, the organization related official circulars in deciding on a suitable protection strategy, mitigation and action plan. This evidence shows that the components of the framework were accepted since they followed standard guidelines of best practices. Framework Stage II involves the processes and activities required during SoE attack risk evaluation and planning. Three processes for stage II were verified and validated by experts to capture the necessary data to assess the framework acceptability, applicability and acceptability of the practices. The following section describes the results and findings of the application.

Framework Stage II involves the processes and activities required during SoE attack risk evaluation and planning. Three processes for stage II were verified and validated by experts to capture the necessary data to assess the framework acceptability, applicability and acceptability of the practices. The following section describes the results and findings of the application. Almost all the processes in Stage II were highly recommended by the experts, based on their applicability and acceptability. The first component, SoE attack risk identification, involved nine (9) steps, and began with a review of the documentation, which was considered a significant, key process that required additional time. The experts strongly affirmed the second step, such as discussing and identifying SoE attack risk issues and areas of concern, which they stipulated as requiring full team participation. Next, the creation of digital evidence security requirement profiles must include a full description of the security requirement (CIA), which was recommended because this would facilitate the measurement of digital evidence information, which would assist in the identification of such assets. A review of information security practices and the risk of SoE attacking vulnerabilities was highly recommended because the experts agreed that this approach assisted in the identification of vulnerabilities in the organization. This leads to the sixth step of creating a profile of SoE attack risk of vulnerabilities for digital evidence, which was deemed an important step and facilitated the prioritization of digital evidence. The experts also strongly advocated the next step of creating a profile for SoE attack risk of management defects, as this approach will assist in identifying the defects, and help investigate security management flaws while strengthening SARM initiatives. Similarly, the eighth step was also recommended because it is highly applicable and acceptable. The expert affirmed that creating a profile for SoE to attack the risk of unexpected change will help assist in the identification of service provider uncertainties and help the organization better prepare for unexpected situations. The final step of consolidating the digital evidence, security requirements, threats and vulnerabilities to produce SoE attack risk descriptions received a high acceptability rating on the grounds that it would provide a clear view of SoE attack risk identification and assist in its organization. The second component, SoE attack risk analysis, involved seven (7) steps, which were rated as mostly highly applicable and acceptable by the experts. The risk analysis workshop preparation was considered moderately applicable and acceptable and was conducted when needed. The next three steps were considered highly acceptable and applicable. The identification of the impact of SoE attack risk on digital evidence requires careful assessment and sufficient resources. Specifically, the third step, such as establishing risk evaluation criteria, was strongly recommended as compulsory and a key step in evaluating risks. Similarly, the experts acknowledged the fourth step, such as evaluating the impact of SoE attack risk on digital evidence, as a compulsory evaluative process. The experts also viewed the process of prioritizing SoE attack risk for each source of risk as compulsory, as this approach will lead to mitigation preparation and plans. A review of these prioritized SoE attack risks must be conducted when necessary, while the seventh step, such as the selection of the mitigation approach—whether to accept, mitigate or transfer—must depend on the nature of the risk and consider the analysis conducted earlier.

The expert's assessment of the third component, such as the SoE attack risk treatment planning and its seven (7) steps, also affirmed its high applicability and acceptability. Generally, the experts viewed SoE attack risk treatment plan workshop preparation as good practice and should be conducted if time is allowed. The next five steps were considered to be highly applicable. First, developing an integrated protection strategy was seen as a key strengthening process, while the third step, developing an integrated protection plan, was recommended as compulsory. The experts commented that the creation of a risk treatment action list must include guidelines on its implementation and a checklist to assist in treatment planning. The next step, to prioritize the execution of the SoE attack risk treatment plan, was also highly applicable and acceptable as it was important to priorities tasks. The preparation of a risk treatment plan document was viewed as compulsory because it helps senior management better understand the plan, which also serves as an important reference document. Finally, the performance of a risk treatment plan for senior management review was assessed as moderately applicable and acceptable and was performed when necessary. Table 6.3 summarizes the key findings of expert judgment for Stage II of the framework.

Table 6.2: Key Summary of Expert Judgment Evaluation – Stage II

Stage II: SoE Attacking Risk Evaluation and Planning (SAREP)				
Framework Components		Applicability	Acceptability	Experts feedback
SAR-EP 1 (SoE attacking risk Identification)	B1 (Review organizational activity)	High	Moderate	Defined in terms of human, technology and process

Framework Components		Applicability	Acceptability	Experts feedback
	B2 (Discuss andidentity SoE attacking risk Issues and Area of Concerns)	Moderate	Moderate	Applicable,requires team member participation
	B3 (Create awareness practice about SoE attacks)	Moderate	Moderate	Provide full description of security requirement (CIA)
	B4 (Create SoE attacking risk of vulnerability profile for digital evidence)	High	Moderate	Assist identification of digital evidence
	B5 (Create SoE attacking risk ofthreat profile for digital evidence)	High	Moderate	Assist identification of service provider uncertainties
	B6 (Create SoE attacking risk of management defects profile for digital evidence)	High	Moderate	Assist identification of SoE attacking risk of management defectsprofile
	B7 (Create SoE attacking risk of unexpected change profile for digital evidence)	High	Moderate	Provide complete description of SoE attacking risk of unexpected change profile for digital evidence

Framework Components		Applicability	Acceptability	Experts feedback
	B 8 (Create SoE attacking risk of digital evidence)	High	High	Define CIA trend of digital evidence
	B9 (Compile and consolidate digital evidence, Security Requirements Threats, Vulnerabilities, to SoE attacking risk description)	Moderate	Moderate	Clear view of SoE attacking risk identification
	Worksheets	Moderate	Moderate	Acceptable the worksheet
SAR-EP 2 (SoE Attacking Risk Analysis)	B10 (Risk Analysis Workshop Preparation)	Moderate	Moderate	Needed when necessary
	B11 (Identify the impact of the SoE Attacking Riskof Threats)	Moderate	Moderate	Needed careful assessment
	B12 (Identify the impact of the SoE Attacking Risk of Vulnerability)	Moderate	Moderate	Key activity for risk evaluation
	B 13 (Identify the impact of the SoE Attacking Riskof management defects)	Moderate	Moderate	Measure impact against digital evidence

Framework Components		Applicability	Acceptability	Experts feedback
	B14 (Identify the impact of the SoE Attacking Riskof unexpected change)	Moderate	Moderate	Lead to organize mitigation preparation
	B15 (Review Priority of SoEAttacking Risk)	High	Moderate	As and when required
	B16 (Selection of Mitigation Approach accept or mitigate or transfer)	High	Moderate	Depend onnature of risk
	Worksheets	Moderate	Moderate	Acceptable but simplified the worksheet
SAREP 3(SoE Attacking Risk Treatment Planning)	B17 (SoE Attacking Risk Treatment planworkshop Preparation)	Moderate	Moderate	Must be clearly identity the digital evidence in the organization
	B18 (Develop an Integrated Protection Strategy)	Moderate	Moderate	SoE attacking risk management practice
	B19 (Develop an Integrated mitigation Plan)	Moderate	Moderate	Consider the technology, human and process in the organization
	B 20 (Create Risk Treatment Action List)	Moderate	Moderate	Carefully consider the SoE attacking risk in the organization

Framework Components		Applicability	Acceptability	Experts feedback
	B21 (PrioritizeSoE AttackingRisk Treatment Plan Execution)	Moderate	High	Carefully consider the SoE attacking risk treatment plan in the organization
	B22 (Prepare Risk Treatment Plan Documentand Presentation forSenior Management)	Moderate	Moderate	Documentation should be clear
	B23 (Conduct Risk Treatment Plan Presentation forSenior Management Review)	Moderate	Moderate	Senior management actually decide whattype of prevention technique they should use to their organization
	Worksheet	Moderate	Moderate	Depend on the organizations

As part of the evaluation process, a review of related documents provided SARAT with a clear understanding from a conceptual view of the necessary input to identify the inherent risk of an SoE attack. Systems-related and operational user manuals, the organization's digital evidence storage policy, the service provider's information security policies and the enterprise network design architecture are among the major documents reviewed to identify SoE attack risk. SARAT discusses related issues with members, the organization and service providers to identify areas of concern. The experts emphasized that the organization's SARAT team should specify their areas of concern, while the service provider should provide feedback. Additionally, creating the digital evidence security requirement profile was required to identify related digital evidence confidentiality, integrity and availability. This component of the framework was suggested to be a critical process in managing SoE attack risk by experts. The experts also strongly verified and validated that the

SARAT required creating an SoE attack risk profile of threats for digital evidence for the organization. This profile allows the SARAT to compile and consolidate the properties of the risk of the threat factors being attacked by the SoE. One of the experts provided examples of several SoE attack risks of threats required to answer the following questions (SoE attack risk of threats – unauthorized access to digital evidence such as national -level exam question papers):

Asset: Name of digital evidence (Exam Question Papers)
Access: Type of access to the Exam Question Papers (Mobile Aps, Web page)
Actor: Persons who exploit the SoE attack risk of threats (internal/external)
Motives: Collect the digital version of exam question papers (Deliberate)
Outcome: Effect showing the weakness of the organization (disclosure of the weakness of theorganizational security)
Impact: Bad impact (organizational reputation)

According to the experts, the inclusion of the SoE attack risk of vulnerability profiles for digital evidence creation in the framework provides a clear view of vulnerability-related activitiesin the organization. In reviewing current information security practices for preventing SoE attacks,the experts attest that the creation of this profile allows the SARAT to compile and consolidate theproperties of the risk of vulnerability factors being attacked by the SoE. For example, before creating a vulnerability profile for the network service provider. The key classes of SoE attack risk of vulnerability of components related to digital evidence, such as software or application vulnerability, hardware or physical device vulnerabilities and telecommunication or media of communication transmission, had to be identified. The following questions were asked (SoE attack risk of vulnerabilities – network service provider):

- Asset: Name of digital evidence (personal data)
- Key Classes: SoE attack risk of the vulnerability class (software and telecommunication)
- Vulnerability Component: Software Application (Code Defects)
- Outcome: Lost or Destruction (Unreasonable Telco charges because of code defects)
- Impact: Reputation of the organization initiator and Telco companies,

monetary losses to systemusers, high expenses of legal attorney and payment for reputation damage by Telco companies.

By creating the SoE attack risk Management Defect (Mgt_d), SARAT can think of the possibility of defects when managing the risk of SoE attack in the organization. Through the expert judgment exercise, the SARAT was required to identify sources of SoE attack risks of management defects for digital evidence. The source of defects could originate from related persons, processes or technology. Other relevant sources of defects could also be identified, and their description was provided in the SoE attack risk of management defect profile (Mgt_d). Creating the (Mgt_d) required answering these questions for business process recovery defects:

- Asset: Name of digital evidence (personal data)
- Source of SoE attacking risk Management Defect: Network Communication Technology (Business Process failures or recovery)
- Outcome: Interruptions (Business Process)
- Impact: Business process reliability, and user confidence to in the service.

Similarly, creating a profile to of the SoE attack risk of unexpected change or uncertainty in the service provider (Unxch) also gives the SARAT another different dimension to consider. An evaluation of its applicability and acceptability by experts also showed that creating this kind of profile contributes to additional efforts in minimizing potential SoE attack risk. Specifically, creating the "Unxch" required answering the following question (Unxch – Technological Changes):

- Asset: Name of digital evidence (personal data)
- Source of the risk of unexpected change caused by SoE attacks: Technological changes (development platform and system integration)
- Outcome: Interruption of the business process.
- Impact: Wastage of organization investment and time on the business process.

At the end of the process of identifying the risk of SoE attack, all the profiles were consolidated to create a profile of the risk of SoE attack, together with digital evidence security requirements. All the experts commented that the consolidation of all the profiles from multiple types of profiles allows analysts to view multiple dimensions of SoE attack risk. Therefore, managing SoE attack risks becomes more systematic and more effective. Generally, the worksheets prepared for this framework component are sufficient to capture the data and input foridentifying the risk of SoE attacks.

Expert Judgment Results: The risk management framework component is logical but depends on organizational activity. SoE attack risk analysis for the organization. Analyses of SARs focus on the probability and impact of risk. Before evaluating the impact. SARAT is required to establish risk evaluation criteria. SARAT uses these criteria to measure and evaluate the impact on the organization. The main reason for analyzing SoE attack risk is to prioritize the risks to enable an appropriate mitigation plan to take place. This requirement was also confirmed by experts based on their responses and other supporting documents.

- SoE attacking risk of threats - Unauthorized access to digital evidence such as the National LevelExamination Question.
- SoE Attacking Risk of Vulnerabilities -— Network Service Provider.
- SoE attack risk of management defects (Mgt_d) - Business process recovery defects
- SoE attack risk of unexpected change (Unxch) - Technological changes.

The mitigation approach to handling unauthorized access to digital evidence was through strengthening the processes and procedures of identity management and database user accounts. Mitigation approaches include seeking legal resources to address network service provider vulnerabilities of source code that cause monetary losses to users. To minimize the risk of management defects such as recovery failures at the data center,the business continuity plan (BCP) should be revised more frequently to identify defects. Technology changes in service provider solutions can sometimes be costly to absorb. Therefore, we need to adapt to this unexpected change or uncertainty when attempting to prevent SoE attacks.

Expert judgment results: The risk of treating planning for the organization according to the SoE attack results from the experts' evaluation of the framework components demonstrate that a well -prepared SoE attack risk in the treatment plan determines its successful execution. Therefore,a workshop to streamline all related mitigation plans is important. This workshop will enable the involved parties to contribute their thoughts on preparing the plan for risk treatment involving SoE attacks. The output of the workshop can be used to develop an Integrated Protection Strategy (IPS) and Integrated Mitigation Plan (IMP) based on the risk identification and analysis results. Among the experts who were directly involved in organizational activities, but specific risks, such as challenges managing service provider uncertainty, differed. The proposed framework, which suggested that a risk treatment action list (RTAL) should be clearly defined and that the execution of the action should be prioritized wisely, was also confirmed by experts. SoE attack risk treatment planning should be documented and presented to senior management. Therefore, any arising issues that arise regarding the implementation of protection strategies, mitigation plans or risk treatment action plans are clearly explained. The purpose of this activity is to bridge the understanding among SARAT and senior management parties. The experts also commented that the communication gap among different levels of staff presents important issues that need to be resolved to ensure that the success of the treatment plan. Therefore, its planning should be well documented and understood by all related persons involved in the organization. Generally, worksheets prepared for this framework component are sufficient to capture data and input for SoEattack risk identification.

The Framework Stage III involves the processes and activities required during the implantation of the treatment plan for the organization. Three processes were reviewed by the experts to capture the necessary data to assess the framework acceptability. The following sectiondescribes the results and findings from the expert verification and validation of Stage III in the confirmatory study. In essence, the final stage of the SARM framework was highly recommendedby experts. The first component of the SoE attack risk Treatment Execution-comprised 3 steps, the first being briefing the SARAT - approved version of the SoE attack risk Treatment Plan. This approach was highly recommended because it could provide greater understanding and educe miscommunication among team members. Second, preparation for risk treatment execution was considered to be a normal practice, and the execution of the risk treatment action plan ultimately required great caution. The experts forewarned that the execution may differ from the plan, that the team had to be aware of changes in the plan and that the execution must adhere to the prioritylist. The second component of this stage is SoE attack risk treatment monitoring, which comprises three steps acquiring data for tracking the progress of the action plan, analyzing the progress of action items and risk indicator data and reporting the progress of the analyzed action plan and risk indictor data. All these, according to the experts, were valid methods if sufficient information wasobtained. The third phase, SoE attack risk treatment control, comprises three highly recommendedsteps. The experts viewed the first step, analyzing risk treatment performance and risk data, as crucial for measuring the performance of the treatment plan, while the second step, making decisions about changes in the treatment action plan, must consider the present treatment plan. Thefinal step of executing new decision changes on the treatment action plan was rated as moderatelyapplicable and included starting with an evaluation of the risk indicator. Table 6.4 summarizes thekey findings of expert judgment for Stage III of the framework.

Table 6.3: Key Summary of Expert Judgment Evaluation – Stage III

Stage III: SoE attacking risk Monitor and Control				
Framework Components		**Applicability**	**Acceptability**	**Experts Feedback**
SAR-MC 1 (SoE attacking risk Treatment execution)	C1 (Briefing the SARAT approved version of SoE attacking risk Treatment Plan)	Moderate	High	Provides understanding about the execution plan
	C2 (Prepare For Risk Treatment Execution)	High	Moderate	Common practice
	C3 Execute Risk Treatment Action Plan)	High	Moderate	Execution of treatment depend on priorities of risk
	Worksheets	Moderate	Moderate	Depend on the organization

Framework Components		Applicability	Acceptability	Experts Feedback
SARMC 2 (SoE attacking risk of treatment monitoring)	C4 (Acquire Data Tracking The Progress Of action Plan)	Moderate	Moderate	Need Sufficient information
	C5 (Analyze the progress of action items and risk indicator data)	Moderate	Moderate	Need Sufficient information
	C6 (Report analyzed Action plan progress and risk indicator data)	Moderate	Moderate	Need Sufficient information
	Worksheets	Moderate	Moderate	Depend on the organization
SARMC 3 (SoE attacking risk of Treatment Control)	C7 (Analyzing Risk Treatment Performance And Risk Data)	Moderate	Moderate	Applicable and practical
	C8 (Making Decision About Changes in Treatment Action Plan)	Moderate	Moderate	Consider Existing Treatment Action plan

Framework Components		Applicability	Acceptability	Experts Feedback
	C9 (Execute New Decision Changes in treatment action plan)	Moderate	Moderate	Evaluate The indicator of risk
	Worksheets	Moderate	Moderate	Logical but depend on the organization

Expert Judgment Results: To increase the risk of attack during treatment execution for theorganization, it is necessary to execute the SoE attack risk during treatment, and that would be necessary to clarify the roles of each team member in addition to individual skills and experiences.Briefing the SARAT and other related teams on the approved version of the SoE attack risk treatment provided a picture of the actual treatment work. Before the execution of the treatment plan, necessary preparations were needed.

Expert Judgment Results: The SoE attack risk of treatment monitoring for the organization results from the experts' judgment verification and validation confirmed that the SoE attack risk treatment and monitoring are important in the process of mitigating the SoE attack risk of for the organization. SARAT was used to measure the effectiveness of specific treatments or action plans. The progress of treatment plans was monitored using the risk treatment action plan item performance worksheet. This worksheet captures the success criteria for each risk treatment action item. The performance can be measured from the beginning, that is, from the onset of the incident to the onset of the incident. Then, the treatment was executed, and the results were ultimately reported to the respective managers. The experts strongly agreed that detailed reports of the risk treatment progress could case future processes of controlling SoE attack risk, particularly when measured from the beginning, that is, from responding to the risk incident related to the SoE attack. These investigations indicated the risk of new SoE attacks. If this happens, changes to the current risk treatment plan are needed. For some extreme cases, new identification of risks ensues, and the entire risk evaluation and planning process changes. Analyzing and compiling the progress of risk treatment action could contribute to building a comprehensive knowledge repository. Eventually, the creation of an intelligent knowledge repository managing SoE, attack risk could assist information security experts in improving information security management for the prevention technique of SoE attacks and supporting organizational success.

Expert Judgment Results: The purpose of the risk treatment control process is to make informed, timely and effective decisions about corrective measures or changes in current risk treatment plans and action lists, if necessary. Generally, experts verify the importance of such a component because it can affect the entire allocation of resources in managing SoE attack risk, moreover, the risk indicator trend, deviation and abnormality need to be unalloyed in SARAT. The purpose of this analysis is to provide supporting evidence for decisions to control treatment risk execution or plans. To manage Management senior management decisions in Changing the course of SoE attack risk treatment, the change register for senior management decisions was used. The worksheet registers records each senior management decision, risk indicator, action plan change description and rationale for the decision. Generally, the worksheets prepared for this framework component are sufficient to capture the data and input for the risk identification of SoE attacks.

6.4. Supplementary Findings: Organizational risk of SoE attacks

SoE attack risk issues are the most important when dealing with the confidentiality, integrity and availability of digital evidence. An information security expert ensures that the infrastructure is equipped with security features to prevent the intrusion of irresponsible individuals. Moreover, data security is provided to ensure that services do not compromise the safety of consumer data and government agencies. Digital evidence can be accessed only by authorized users, and a verification process is required to determine the authenticity of the evidence.

The expert judgment confirmed the introduction of the five SoE attack risk factors (SoE attack risk of threats, SoE attack risk of vulnerabilities, SoE attack risk of management defects, SoE attack risk of unexpected changes and SoE attack risk of digital evidence) into the framework. Thus, the entire process of managing the risk of attack by the SoE considers these information security risk factors. Through several meetings with personnel, it was found that a limited comprehensive SoE attack risk management approach was used to represent the entire process of the organization. Therefore, the introduction of the proposed framework served as an additional approach for integrating

SARM into organizational activities. The following are the findings on the organization's SoE attack risk management practices through expert judgment.

- SARM focuses on the operational level of organizational activities.
- The preliminary SoE attack risk of study for the organization began when it was awarded to the service provider.
- No specific team for SoE attack risk assessment was presented.
- Insufficient monitoring of service providers' (vendors') SoE attack risk of management practicesand operations.
- SoE attack risk management covered only threats and vulnerability risk factors.

Accordingly, the experts agreed that the introduction of the framework is significant and could improve how the organization manages SoE attack risk. Through the expert judgment method, overlooked or unobserved SoE attack risk management efforts were highlighted. Highlighting these security risk management efforts allowed the organizations to improve the way they handled the security of digital evidence in their organizational activities. Before the SoE attack risk study was conducted, the involved SoE attack risk analysis team (SARAT) was required to gain full senior management support. This is the most essential requirement. Thus, structured and systematic procedures should be created to support senior management involved in the organization. The expert judgment observed that communication barriers between professionals and information security experts and senior management can pose challenges to SoE attack risk analysis teams. Therefore, without effective communication, senior management could interpret the research and assessment of the risks differently. Other unobserved practices include most of the SoE attack risk management efforts starting at the end of the organization (during the ongoing monitoring phase). In other words, the organization focused solely on SoE attack risk management efforts during the operational phase. It was also suggested by expert judgment that the organization may be dealing with several constraints in implementing SARAT and, consequently, may omit some of the SoE attack risk management practices. Time and resource constraints were the main factors causing the omission of some of the processes. Therefore, only the most relevant SoE attack risk management activities were conducted on a demand basis. These were mostly responsive actions to risks and remedial action on the impact of the risk in business continuity. The expert feedback also highlighted that there was insufficient dedicated team members to focus on SoE attack risk evaluation and that information security experts were not directly involved in the organization. Additionally, it was suggested that organizations may not have specific approaches for managing SoE attack risk, as they currently focus only on threats and vulnerability risk factors. Therefore, the introduction of the approach to managing the three other additional risk factors mentioned earlier in the study is most likely significant for improving practices to minimize risk occurrences and negative impacts on the organization. Subsequently, the refined SARM when effectively enforced, a framework can act as an enabler for increasing the quality of the organization.

The objective of the framework is to manage SoE attack risk in the organization. The inclusion of the theoretical foundation and empirical and exploratory validation make this framework reliable and robust. Even when all these constructs are included in the SARM framework, their impact on organizations remains unknown since the previous framework has combined all the above-mentioned constructs. Consequently, using an expert judgment method, the framework was verified and validated in a scientific and structured manner. Hence, current SoE attack risk management was discovered, and several unobserved SoE attack risk management practices were highlighted, with further improvements recommended. The results of the confirmatory study also augment the assumption that the introduction of the framework, together with top management support, appears to be an important complement. Increased awareness of the relevance and workability of the SARM framework will ensure top management support, thus consolidating its introduction and enhancing its effectiveness.

Without a dedicated framework and guidelines, significant stages, processes and activities in SARM for organizational practices could be omitted, thus hampering the achievement of optimum benefit. Supplementary findings were also gathered from this study. Even though organizations have tried to apply SoE attack risk management, some of the overlooked challenges should be overcome to improve SARM practices. Furthermore, investing time and effort in structured SARM practices, as proposed in the framework, will allow organizations to fully reap the benefit. The next chapter concludes the results of the study and suggests potential research in SARM for the organization.

References

Abawajy, J. (2014). User preference of cyber security awareness delivery methods. Behavior & Information Technology, 33 (3), 237-248.

Adrian. M. (2017). Running the Risk IT – More Perception and Less Probabilities in Uncertain Systems. Information & Computer Security, 25 (3), 45-59.

Alberts, C., & Carol, W. (2007). Considering Operational Security Risk during System Development, IEEE Security & Privacy, 5 (1), 30 - 35.

Alfonsi, C., Rabiti, D., Mandelli, J.J., Cogliati, R.A., Kinoshita. (2013). Raven As A Tool For Dynamic Probabilistic Risk Assessment: Software Overview. International Conference on Mathematics and Computational Methods Applied to Nuclear Science & Engineering, 5 (4), 456- 467.

Algarni, A., Xue, Y., & Chan, T. (2017). An empirical study on the susceptibility to social engineering in social networking sites: the case of Facebook. European Journal of Information Systems, 26 (6), 661-687.

Amanda Andress. (2003). Surviving Security: How to integrate People, Process and Technology, 2nd ed., Auerbach Publications.

Anita, V., & Les Labuschagne. (2009). A framework for comparing different information security risk analysis methodologies. ACM Digital Library, 28 (4), 651-667.

Ana. F., Gabriele. L. (2016). An analysis of social engineering principles in effective phishing. IEEE, 3 (5), 33-49.

APCERT. (2014). Computer Security Incident Response Teams (CSIRTs) Report, 2014. Appin Security Group. (2017). Information Security Management Practices Report.

Applegate, S.D. (2009). A Global Perspective of Social Engineering: Hacking the Wetware. Information Security Journal: A Global Perspective, 18 (1), 40-46.

Ayesha. M. & Muhammad. M. (2013). Security Framework for Cloud Computing Environment: A Review. Journal of Emerging Trends in Computing and Information Sciences, 3 (3), 91-101.

Bill. G. & Valerie. T. (2016). Building an information security awareness program: Defending against social engineering and technical threats. Elsevier. Copyright.

Bob. B., Ellen. M., Dan. G. (2005). Information security is information risk management. Proceedings of the 2001 workshop on New security, 4 (1), 97-104.

Brill. A., Pollit, M., & Whitcomb, C. M. (2013). The Evolution of Computer Forensic Best Practices: An Update on Programs and Publications. Journal of Digital Forensic Practice, 1 (1), 3- 11.

Buskirk, E.V. & Liu, V.T. (2006). Digital Evidence: Challenging the Presumption of Reliability. Journal of Digital Forensic Practice, 1 (1), 19-26.

Cheung, S. K. S. (2014). Information Security Management for Higher Education Institutions. Intelligent Data analysis and its Applications, 1 (2), 55-68.

Christopher. H. (2018). Social Engineering: The Science of Human Hacking. John Wiley & Sons.

Christopher. H. (2013). Managing Information Security Risks: The Octave Approach. Addison- Wesley Longman Publishing.

Clif A. Ericson (2016). Hazard analysis techniques for system safety. John Wiley & Sons.

Cojazzi. G (1996). Preliminary Requirements for a Knowledge Engineering Approach to Expert Judgment Elicitation in Probabilistic Safety Assessment. International Conference on Probabilistic Safety Assessment and Management, 24 (2), 491-498.

Cojazzi G., Keejam (2003). Benchmark exercise on expert judgment techniques. Nuclear Engineering and Design, 21 (1), 211-221.

Cooke & Goossens (2010). TU Delft expert judgment data base. Reliability Engineering & System Safety, 93 (5), 657-674.

Cooke. M., & Abigail, R. (2017). Cross validation for the classical model of structured expert judgment. Reliability Engineering & System Safety, 163 (1), 109-120.

Cooke, M., Julie. C., Ryana.T. (2012). Quantifying information security risks using expert judgment elicitation. Computers & Operations Research, 39 (4), 774-784.

Cojazzi & G. Fogli.D (2001). Benchmark Exercise on Expert Judgment Techniques in PSA Level 2. Nuclear Engineering and Design, 1 (3), 211-221.

Conway. B.A. (2010). Calibrating Expert Assessments of Advanced Aerospace Technology Adoption Impact. Dominion University Journal, 3 (1), 22-29.

Cremonini, M. & Nizovtsev, D., (2009). Risks and Benefits of Signaling Information System Characteristics to Strategic Attackers. Journal of Management Information Systems, 26 (3), 241- 274.

D'Arcy, J., Herath, T.& Shoss, M.K. (2014). Understanding Employee Responses to Stressful Information Security Requirements: A Coping Perspective. Journal of Management Information Systems, 31 (2), 285-318.

Daniel, D., Yuval, E. (2016). A model of the information security investment decision- making process. Computers & Security, 63 (4), 1-13.

Donn. B. (2013). Toward a New Framework for Information Security. John Wiley & Sons.

Duff, A. S. (2007) Social Engineering in the Information Age. An International Journal, 21 (1), 67- 71.

Dwyer. F., Schurr, P., & Ohior, S. (1999). Developing Buyer—Seller Relationship. Journal of Marketing, 51 (2), 11-19.

Edward. H. (2015). Implementing the ISO/IEC 27001 Information Security Management System Standard. The ACM Digital Library, 11 (2), 109-120.

Ekelhart. A., Fenz. S., & Neubauer.T. (2009). AURUM: A Framework for

Information Security Risk Management. System Sciences (HICSS), Annual Hawaii International Conference, 4 (2), 30- 39.

Ekelhart. A., Fenz. S., & Neubauer. T. (2009). Ontology-Based Decision Support for Information Security Risk Management. ICONS International Conference, 2 (1), 79-87.

Eisenhardt, K. M. (1989). Agency Theory: An Assessment and Review, Academy of Management. The Academy of Management Review, 14 (1), 57-61.

Eyong. K. (2014). Recommendations for information security awareness training for college students. Information Management & Computer Security, 3 (2), 33-45.

Eloff, M., & Solms, S. (2014). Information Security Management: A Hierarchical Framework for Various Approaches. Computers & Security, 19 (3), 243-256.

Fan. W., Kevin. L. (2017). Social Engineering: I-E based Model of Human Weakness for Attack and Defense Investigations. Computer Network and Information Security, 9 (1), 1 - 11.

Feriel. D., Selmin. N. (2014). A benchmarking framework for methods to design flexible business processes. Software Process: Improvement and Practice, 12 (1), 51-63.

Georg. D. (2014). ISO/IEC 27000, 27001 and 27002 for Information Security Management. Journal of Information Security, 4 (2), 92-100.

Gewald. H., Wollemscbcr, K. & Weitzel, T (2014). The Influence of perceived risks on banking managers intention to organizational business process — A Study of German banking and finance industry. Journal of Electronic Commerce Research, 7 (2), 78-96.

Gerben. S., Peter. E., Margareta. W., Gerard. G. (2015). Managing Risk and Resilience. Academy of Management Journal, 58 (4), 305-314.

Gita Radhakrisna. (2014). Digital evidence in Malaysia. Journal of Digital Evidence and Electronic Signature Law Review, 31 (5), 220-240.

Gregory. R., Hancock. L., Stapleton. R. (2018). The Reviewer's Guide to Quantitative Methods in the Social Sciences. Taylor & Francis Group.

Gurpreet. D., Romilla. Syed. & Cristiane. P. (2016). Interpreting information security culture: An organizational transformation case study. Computers & Security, 56 (2), 63- 69.

Hartini. S., Zaiton. H. (2013). The application of the digital signature law in securing internet banking: Some preliminary evidence from Malaysia. Procedia Computer Science, 3 (2), 248-253.

Heidi. W. & Maumita. B. (2016). Countering Social Engineering Through Social Media: An Enterprise Security Perspective. Journal of Computational Collective Intelligence, 14 (2), 54-64.

Ian Mann. (2018). Hacking the human: social engineering techniques and security countermeasures. Taylor & Francis Group.

Isabella McMurray & Charlotte Brownlow. (2016). SPSS explained. Taylor & Francis Group.

Jacques, B & Rossouw V. A cyclic approach to business continuity planning. Information Management & Computer Security, 12 (4), 328-337.

Joe. F., Christian. M., & Marko. S. (2012). PLS-SEM: Indeed a Silver Bullet. Journal of Marketing Theory and Practice, 19 (2), 139-152.

Joe. F., Hair. J., Marko. S., Lucas. H., & Volker. G. (2015). Partial least squares structural equation modeling (PLS-SEM): An emerging tool in business research. European. Business Review, 7 (2), 79-89.

Joseph. F., Tomas. M. (2016). A Primer on Partial Least Squares Structural Equation Modeling (PLS-SEM). SAGE Publications.

Juhani. A., Kari. J., Jorma. K., Ilkka. K. (2013). Integrating ISO/IEC 27001 and other Managerial Discipline Standards with Processes of Management in Organizations, 6 (2), 73-89.

Justin, W., Eggstaff, T., Mazzuchi S. (2014). The Development of Progress Plans Using a Performance-Based Expert Judgment Model to Assess Technical Performance and Risk. Systems Engineering, 22 (6), 471-484.

Halliday Badenhorst. S. and Solms, V. (2003). A Business Approach to Effective Information Technology Risk Analysis and Management. Information Management and Computer Security, 4 (1), 19-31.

Harold. F., Micki. k. (2013). Information security management handbook. Taylor & Francis Group.

Harwood, I. A. (2006). Confidentiality constraints with mergers and acquisitions. Gaining insights through a 'bubble' metaphor. British Journal of Management, 1 (7), 347-359.

Hartini, S.& Zaiton, H. (2011). The application of the digital signature law in securing internet banking: Some preliminary evidence from Malaysia. Procedia Computer Science, 3 (1), 248-253.

Hawkins, S. M., Yen, D.C., and Chou, D.C. (2000). Disaster Recovery Planning. A Strategy for Data Security. Information Management and Computer Security, 8 (3), 222- 230.

Heidi. W., Maumita B., Rafiqul I. (2014). Social Engineering through Social Media: An Investigation on Enterprise Security. International Conference on Applications and Techniques in Information Security, 5 (3), 243-255.

Hinson, G. (2011), Handbook of Research on Social and Organizational Liabilities in Information Security. Taylor & Francis Group.

Hinson G. (2013). Information Security Management Metrics: A Definitive Guide to Effective Security Monitoring and Measurement. The EDP Audit, Control, and Security Newsletter, 43 (3), 9-15.

Hinson, G. (2007). The State of IT Auditing in 2007. The EDP Audit, Control, and Security Newsletter, 36 (1), 13-31.

Hinson, G. & Brotby, W.K. (2016). PRAGMATIC Security Metrics: Applying Metametrics to Information Security. CRC Press, Taylor & Francis Group.

Hinson, G. (2008). Social Engineering Techniques, Risks, and Controls. The EDP Audit, Control, and Security Newsletter, 37 (4), 32-46.

Jean Boltz (2015). Informational Security Risk Assessment: Practices of Leading Organizations. Diane Publishing.

Jeb.W., Atif.A., Maynard.G. (2015). A situation awareness model for information security risk management. Computers & Security, 44 (2), 1-15.

Joseph F. & Tomas. M. (2016). A Primer on Partial Least Squares Structural Equation Modeling (PLS-SEM). SAGE Publications.

Joseph F., Jeffrey. R., Marko. S. & Christian. M. (2019). When to use and how to report the results of PLS-SEM. European Business Review, 25 (3), 456-469.

John Gerring. (2015). Social science methodology: A criterial framework. Cambridge University Press.

K. Papadaki. K., & Nineta. P. (2015). Towards a Systematic Approach for Improving Information Security Risk Management Methods. IEEE 18th International Symposium on Personal, Indoor and Mobile Radio Communications, 4 (2), 55-61.

Katharina. K., Heidelinde. H., Markus. H., Edgar. W. (2015). Advanced social engineering attacks. Journal of Information Security and Applications, 22 (3), 113-122.

Kebande. V. R. & Venter, H. S. (2018). Novel digital forensic readiness technique in the cloud environment. Australian Journal of Forensic Sciences, 50 (5), 552-591.

Kebande, V. R. & Venter, H. S. (2018). On digital forensic readiness in the cloud using a distributed agent-based solution: issues and challenges. Australian Journal of Forensic Sciences, 50 (2), 209-238.

Kim, E.B. (2013). Information Security Awareness Status of Business College: Undergraduate Students. Information Security Journal: A Global Perspective, 22 (4), 171- 179.

Kliem. R. (2008). Managing the Risks of Offshore IT Development. The EDP Audit, Control, and Security Newsletter, 32 (4), 12-20.

Korchenko, O., Vasiliu, Y. & Gnatyuk, S. (2014). Modern quantum technologies of information security against cyber-terrorist attacks. Journal of Aviation, 14 (2), 58-69.

Leandre. R., Fabrigar & Duane. T. (2014). Exploratory Factor Analysis. Oxford University Press. Linstone. M. (1999), The Delphi Method Techniques and Applications. Addison Wesley.

Louis. A. (2010). What's Wrong with Risk Matrices? Wiley Online Library, 28 (2), 497 - 512.

Logan, M. S. (2000). Using Agency Theory to Design Successful Organizational Relationship. International Journal of Logistics Management, 11 (2), 21-31.

Lund, S., Den Braber, F., Stolen, K. & Vraalscn; F. (2015). A UML profile for the identification and analysis of security risks during structured brainstorming, STEF Technical Journal, 4 (3), 220- 234.

MAMPU (2019). The Malaysian Public Sector Information Security High-Level Risk Assessment (HiLRA) Guide. National Library of Malaysia.

Marian, C., Karen, R., Stephen, M, & Conor O'Brien. (2017). A Framework for Information Security Governance and Management. IT Professional, 18 (2), 22 – 30.

Maria. E., Garcia. U., Josefina. L., Murillo. L. (2017). Application of the Delphi Method for the Analysis of the Factors Determining Social Entrepreneurship, 9 (1), 43-66.

Malaysian Cyber Security (2018), The Malaysian public and private Sector Information Security Risk Assessment Methodology.

Manes, G. W. & Downing, E. (2010). What Security Professionals Need to Know About Digital Evidence. Information Security Journal: A Global Perspective, 19 (3), 124- 131.

Manske.K. (2008). An introduction to social engineering. Information Systems Security, 9 (5), 1-7.

Malacaria, P. (2007). Assessing security threats of looping constructs. Proc. ACM Symposium on Principles of Programming Language, 3 (1), 56-67.

Malacaria, P. & Chen (2008). Lagrange Multipliers and Maximum Information Leakage in Different Observational Models. Proceedings of the third ACM SIGPLAN workshop on Programming languages and analysis for security Journal, 5 (1), 135-146.

Malhotra. N K (1996), Marketing Research and Applied Orientation. 4th Edition, New York. Prentice Hall.

Markus. H., Stewart. K., Marcus. N. (2009). Towards Automating Social Engineering Using Social Networking Sites. International Conference on Computational Science and Engineering, 8 (1), 65-77.

Menezes. A., van. P. &Vanstone. S. (1997). Handbook of Applied Cryptography. CRC Press.

Mingscong Ju, Scoksoo Kim, and Tai-Noon Kim. (2017). A Study on Digital Media Security by Hopfield Neural Network. Advances in Neural Networks, 5 (1), 140-153.

Marshall, K., Matthew, S. &Philip, K. (2018). Cyber Risk Management for Critical Infrastructure: A Risk Analysis Model and Three Case Studies. Wiley Online Library, 38 (2), 226-241.

Michael. J. (2007). Information Management System: The Organizational Dimension. Oxford University Press.

Muhammad, S., Maimoona, S., Alain, F., Norizan, J. (2018). Impact of service quality on customer satisfaction in Malaysia airlines: A PLS-SEM approach. Journal of Air Transport Management, 67 (1), 169-180.

Mohamed. G., Sophia. F., Hicham. M., Adil. S. (2016). Information Security Risk Assessment — A Practical Approach with a Mathematical Formulation of Risk. International Journal of Computer Applications, 103 (8), 89-99.

Mustaruddin, S., Norhayah Z. & Rusnah M. (2010). Malaysian Corporate social responsibility disclosure and its relation on institutional ownership. Managerial Auditing Journal, 2 (6), 349-350.

Manske, K. (2006). An Introduction to Social Engineering. Information Systems Security, 9 (5), 1- 7.

Mohamed, N., Nawawi, A., Ismail, I. S., Ahmad., S.A., Azmi, N.A. & Zakaria, N.B. (2013). Cyber fraud challenges and the analysts competency: Evidence from digital forensic department of Cyber Security Malaysia. Recent Trends in Social Sciences -Proceedings of the 2nd International Congress on Interdisciplinary Behavior and Social Sciences, 3 (2), 581-583.

Molok, N.N.A., Ahmad, A. & Chang, S. (2018). A case analysis of securing organisations against information leakage through online social networking. International Journal of Information Management, 43 (4), 351-356.

Myyry, L., Siponen, M., Pahnila, S. & Vartiainen, A. (2009). What levels of moral reasoning and values explain adherence to information security rules? An empirical study. European Journal of Information Systems, 18 (2), 126-139.

Nabie. Y., Conteh P., Schmick. (2016). Cybersecurity: risks, vulnerabilities and countermeasures to prevent social engineering attacks. International Journal of Advanced Computer Research, 23 (6), 345-360.

Nader. S., Safa. R. & Solms. L. (2016). Human aspects of information security in organizations. Computer Fraud & Security, 3 (2), 15-18.

Ned. K. (2016). Common method bias in PLS-SEM: A full collinearity assessment approach. International Journal of e-Collaboration, 5 (2), 70-89.

Neeta. S., & Sachin. K. (2014). A Comparative Study on Information Security Risk Analysis Practices. International Journal of Computer Applications, 11 (3), 123-139.

Nikolaos.A., Konstantinos. A., Haralambos. M., Andrew. F. (2017). Decision-Making in Security Requirements Engineering with Constrained Goal Models. Computer Security, 34 (2), 262-280.

Nik.Z., Azlinah. M. & Noor. H. (2010). Information security risk factors: Critical threats vulnerabilities in ICT outsourcing. IEEE, 23 (4), 65-79.

Nik.Z., Azlinah. M. & Noor. H. (2013). ICT Outsourcing Information Security Risk Factors: An Exploratory Analysis of Threat Risks Factor for Critical Project Characteristics. Journal of Industrial and Intelligent Information, 1 (4), 44-59.

Nik. Z., Shekh. A. (2019). Toward Fact- Based Digital Forensic Evidence Collection Methodology. International Journal for Information Security Research (IJISR), 9 (1), 67- 79.

Nik. Z., Shekh. A. (2018). Legal Protection of intellectual property rights (IPR) in Bangladesh. International Journal of Law. Government and Communication, 3 (12), 71- 89.

Nik. Z., Shekh. A. &Tan. T. (2018). Viewpoint of Probabilistic Risk Assessment in Artificial Enabled Social Engineering Attacks. BITARA International Journal of Civilizational Studies and Human Sciences, 1 (4), 32-39.

Nik. Z., Noor. H. & Azlinah. M. (2010). Conceptual Framework on Information Security Risk Management in Information Technology. Journal of Media and Information Warfare, 3 (4), 77 – 104.

Nina Godbole (2017). Information System Security, Security Management, Metrics, Framework and Best Practices. John Wiley & Sons, Inc.

Noor. H., Yap. M., Azlinah. M. (2007) Inherent risks in ICT. Proceeding of the 8th WSEAS Conference, 8 (1), 141 – 146.

Noor. H., Azlinah. M. (2012). Chaos issues on communication in Agile Global Software Development. IEEE Business, 6 (2) 55-68.

Noor. H., Azlinah. M. (2010). IT governance practices model in IT project approval and implementation in Malaysian public sector. IEEE, 12 (1), 442-456.

Noor. H., Azlinah. M. (2010). Information Technology governance practices in Malaysian public sector. IEEE, 2 (1), 44-56.

Otway. H. and Wintcrfeldt, D. von, (1999). Expert judgment in risk analysis and management: Process, context, and pitfalls. The Journal of Risk Analysis, 12 (1), 83-93.

Parker Donn (2014). Toward a New Framework for Information Security, Computer Security Handbook New York: John Wiley & Sons.

Peltier. T. R. (2012). Information Security Risk Analysis. 3rd Edition CRC Press, Taylor & Francis Group.

Peltier, T. R. (2006). Social Engineering: Concepts and Solutions. Information Systems Security, 15 (5), 13-21.

Peltier, T. R. (2016). Information Security Policies, Procedures, and Standards: guidelines for effective information security management. Taylor & Francis Group.

Price Waterhouse Coopers (2010). Information Security Breach Survey. Journal of Current research in computing, 4 (2), 67-73.

Patton, M.Q. (2004). Two Decades of Developments in Qualitative Inquiry: A Personal, Experiential Perspective. Journal of Developmental Child Welfare, 1 (3), 261-283.

Poppo, L. & Zenger. T. (1998). Testing Alternative Theories of the Finn: Transaction Cost, Knowledge-Based, and Measurement Explanations in Information Services. Strategic Management Journal, 19 (9), 853-862.

Posey. C., Roberts. T.& Lowry. P. (2015). The Impact of Organizational Commitment on Insiders' Motivation to Protect Organizational Information Assets. Journal of Management Information Systems, 32 (4), 179-214.

Rahul Singh (2015). Kali Linux Social Engineering - Effectively perform efficient and organized social engineering tests and penetration testing using Kali Linux. Packt Publishing Inc. Ltd.

Rai Kaplan. (2010), A Matter of Trust, Information Security Management, Handbook. 5 Edition.

Rossouw. V., Solms. J. Niekerk. (2014). From information security to cyber security. Computers & Security, 38 (4), 97-102.

Sameer, H., Bharanidharan, S., Ganthan, N., Norbik, B., Azuan, A. (2014). Security risk assessment framework for cloud computing environments. Wiley Online Library, 7 (11), 114-124.

Sandelowski, M. (2013). Focus on Research Method, Combining Qualitative and Quantitative Sampling, Data Collection, and Analysis Techniques in Mixed-Method studies. Research in Nursing and Health, 23 (1), 246-255.

Selcaran, U. (2016). Research Methods for Business, 5rd Edition. New York: John Wiley an Sons.

Shaun. P. & Rossouw. V. (2006). A framework for the governance of information security. Computers & Security, 23 (8), 638-646.

Shekh. A., Nik. Z., Tan. T. (2019). Toward the Data Security and Digital Evidence-based Solution in Bangladesh Perspective, ZULFAQAR International Journal of Defense Science, Engineering & Technology, 21 (1), 20-19.

Shekh. A., Nik. Z., Tan. T. (2019). Towards the Big Data and Digital Evidence Integrity. Journal of Intelek, 14 (1), 56-63.

Shekh. A. (2019). Security of Electronic Mail System, Folio, FTKW Magazine.

Shekh. A. (2018). Mobile Device Security, 1E- Proceeding of the 1st International MedLit Media Literacy for social change conference 2018, 2 (1), 342-350.

Shekh. A., Nik. Z., Tan. T. (2018). An Investigation of AI enabled Social Engineering (SoE) Attacking Impact in Higher Learning Institute: Structural Equation Modeling (SEM) Approach. Journal of Applied & Computational Mathematics, 23 (2), 562-570.

Shekh. A., Nik. Z. (2018). An Exploratory Factor Analysis of AI Enabled Social Engineering (SoE) Attacking Risk in Higher Learning Institute, Journal of Mass Communication & Journalism, 15 (1), 32-40.

Singleton, T. W. & Singleton, A. J. (2014). The Potential for a Synergistic Relationship Between Information Security and a Financial Audit. Information Security Journal: A Global Perspective, 17 (2), 80-86.

Siti Rahayu, S., Robiah Y., Shahrin S. (2014). Malaysian Mapping Process of Digital Forensic Investigation Framework. International Journal of Computer Science and Network Security, 8 (10), 26-35.

Suci. R., Yasmirah. M., Robbi. R & Andysah. P. (2017). Post-Genesis Digital Forensics Investigation. International Journal of Science and Technology, 3 (6), 123-133.

Sumner, M. (2011). Information Security Threats: A Comparative Analysis of Impact, Probability, and Preparedness. Information Systems Management, 26 (1), 2-12.

Sundresan Perumal (2009). Digital Forensic Model Based On Malaysian Investigation Process. International Journal of Computer Science and Network Security, 9 (8), 119- 126.

Suit & Han. (2008). Information System (IS) analysis based on a business model. Journal of Global Information Management, 14 (3), 39-49.

Tim Bedford, Roger M. Cooke. (2015). Probabilistic Risk Analysis: Foundations and Methods, Cambridge University Press.

Todd. F. (2016). Physical Security. Handbook of Information Security Management. Taylor & Francis Group.

Veiga. A. & Eloff. J. (2009). An Information Security Governance Framework. Information Systems Management, 24 (4), 361-372.

Wiebke, A. (2009). Agents, Trojans and tags: The next generation of investigators. International Review of Law, Computers & Technology, 23 (1-2), 99-108.

Yin, R.K. (1984), Case Study Research Design and Method Newbury Park. CA. SAGE Publications.

Yudistira. A., Paolo. G. (2010). Modeling Risk and Identifying Countermeasure in Organizations. International Workshop on Critical Information Infrastructures Security, 4 (3), 55-66.

Appendix

SAREP: SoE ATTACKING RISK IDENTIFICATION WORKSHEET

Introduction

This worksheet was created by the SoE Attacking Risk Analysis Team (SARAT) to document discussions and the results of a brainstorming session conducted during the SoE Attacking Risk Identification Workshop (Workshop 1). This worksheet consists of the following section:

- Section A – SoE Attacking Risk Issues
- Section B – Digital evidence and Rationale
- Section C – Digital Evidence, Source of Potential Threats, Vulnerabilities and Outcomes
- Section D –Organization Digital Evidence Potential Source of Threats, Vulnerabilities andOutcomes Scenario Diagram
- Section E – Digital Evidence Description
- Section F – Digital Evidence Security Requirement Profile
- Section G - SoE Attacking Risk of Threats Profile for Digital Evidence
  - Human Factor Problems
  - Technology/System Problems
  - Other Problems
- Section H – Information Security Practices and the SoE Attacking Risk of Vulnerabilitiesfor Systems of Interest
- Section I – Relevant Key Class Components for SoE Attacking Risk of Vulnerabilities
- Section J – SoE Attacking Risk of Vulnerability Profiles for Digital Evidence
- Section K– SoE Attacking Risk of Management Defect
- Section L – SoE Attacking Risk of Unexpected Change
- Section M- SoE Attacking Risk Profile

ORGANIZATIONAL DESCRIPTION					
Name	**Description**	**Owner**	**User**	**Service Provider**	**Duration**

SECTION A (ACTIVITY B2) SoE ATTACKING RISK ISSUES		
No	**SoE Attacking Risk Issues**	**Severity (How serious the issues?)**
1	Business activity interruptions	
2	Data or information theft (Financial Records)	
3	Information Leakage (Confidential data or reports)	
4	Intellectual Property (IP) Right	
5	Information Privacy (Personal or Organization)	
6	....	

SAREP: SoE ATTACKING RISK IDENTIFICATION WORKSHEET

SECTION B (ACTIVITY) DIGITAL EVIDENCE AND RATIONALE		
No	Digital Evidence	Rationale (provide the reason of your selections)
1	Business & Financial Records	
2	Client's Profiles	
3	Archived Data/Information	
4	Policy & Procedures	
5	Legal & Contract Documents	
6	Database & Data Files	

<table>
<tr><td>7</td><td colspan="2">System Documentation</td><td colspan="2"></td></tr>
<tr><td>8</td><td colspan="2">...</td><td colspan="2"></td></tr>
<tr><td colspan="5">SECTION C (ACTIVITY)
DIGTIAL EVIDENCE, SOURCE OF POTENTIAL THREATS, VULNERABILITIESAND OUTCOMES</td></tr>
<tr><td colspan="2">Information</td><td>Source of SoE attacking risk of threats</td><td>Source of SoE attacking risk of vulnerabilities</td><td>Outcomes</td></tr>
<tr><td colspan="2">Name Of Digital Evidence</td><td>Deliberate or Accidental Human Actor (Internal or External) or System defects or Software defects or unavailable of Malicious Code-Virus, Worm, Trojan Horse, Backdoor, etc) or Other Problem (Power outages or Telecommunication Networking or ISP unavailable, etc)</td><td>Technology or HumanProcess or</td><td>Disclosure of Viewing of Sensitive Information or Modification of Important or Sensitive Information or Destruction or loss of important information, hardware, software etc or Interruption of access to important information, software application.</td></tr>
<tr><td colspan="2">Business & Financial Records</td><td>Deliberate Human Actor</td><td>Technology</td><td>Disclosure</td></tr>
<tr><td colspan="2">.............................
.</td><td>.................................</td><td>........................</td><td>........................
...........</td></tr>
</table>

SAREP: SoE ATTACKING RISK IDENTIFICATION WORKSHEET

SECTION D (ACTIVITY)

ORGANIZATION DIGITAL EVIDENCE POTENTIAL SOURCE OF SoE ATTACKINGRISK OF THREATS AND SoE ATTACKING RISK OF VULNERABILITIES AND OUTCOMES SCENARIO DIAGRAM

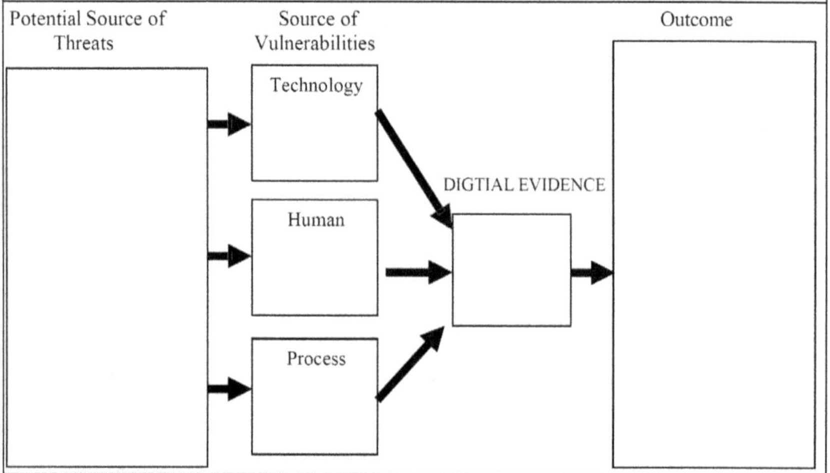

SoE ATTACKING RISK AREAS OF CONCERN SCENARIO

No	SoE Attacking Risk Areas of Concern Scenarios (Please consider digital evidence, sourceof SoE attacking risk of threats, SoE attacking risk of vulnerabilities and outcomes)
1	Disclosure of Business and Financial Record to unauthorized external user through deliberate action caused by internet or Computer Network Security Vulnerabilities
2.	.... of .... to unauthorized.. caused by ....
3.	.... of .... to unauthorized.. caused by ....
4.	.... of .... to unauthorized.. caused by ....

5.	....

SAREP: SoE ATTACKING RISK IDENTIFICATION WORKSHEET

SECTION G (ACTIVITY) SoE ATTACKING RISK OF VULNERABILITY PROFILE FOR DIGITAL EVIDENCE(HUMAN FACTOR PROBLEMS)	
Vulnerability ProfilesName	Please consider how the vulnerability occur? who operate the vulnerability?vulnerability outcomes? Impact?)
Digital Evidence	(name of Digital Evidence)
Nature of vulnerability	

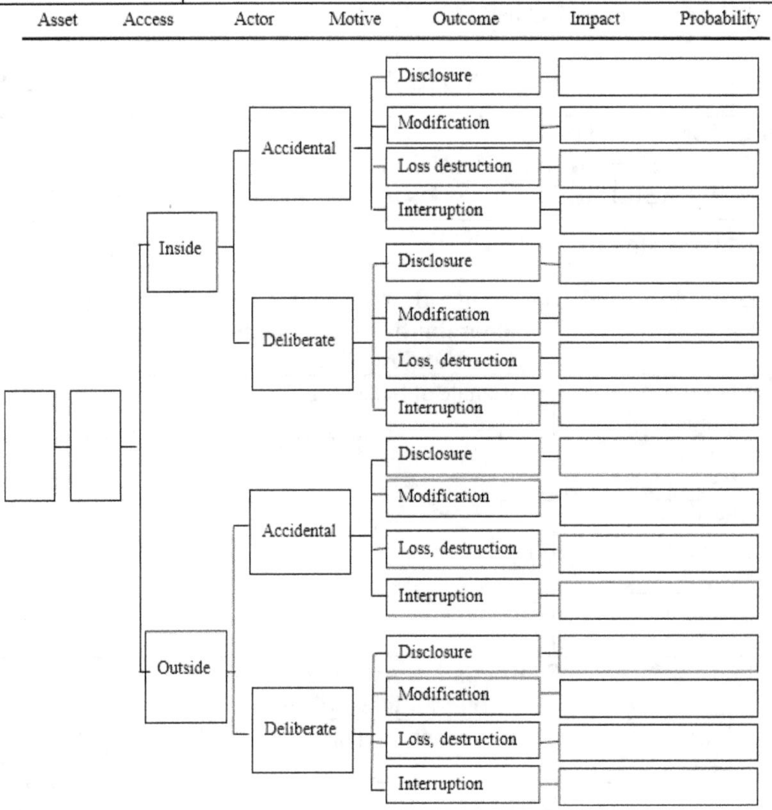

SAREP: SoE ATTACKING RISK IDENTIFICATION WORKSHEET

SECTION G (ACTIVITY) SoE ATTACKING RISK MANAGEMENT PRACTICES AND VULNERABILITIES FOR THEORGANIZATION	
No	Please consider to these questions
1	which system(s) is most closely linked to the digital evidence? In which system(s) is the digital evidencestored and processed?
2	Where outside the system of interest do digital evidence move? Backup system? Off-site storage? other?
3	Based on the digital evidence, which system(s) would be the best target of a vulnerability actor actingdeliberately?
4	What are the natures of vulnerabilities? Technology? Human? Process? What are the key class ofvulnerabilities components?
5	Impact of the vulnerabilities to digital evidence? Impact to organization impact to services? Other?

SAREP: SoE ATTACKING RISK IDENTIFICATION WORKSHEET

SECTION G (ACTIVITY) RELEVANT KEY CLASS COMPONENT FOR SoE ATTACKING RISK OF VULNERABILITIES	
INFORMATION	
Source of SoE Attacking Risk of Vulnerabilities: Technology Vulnerabilities	
Key Classes of Component	Rationale of Selection
Software or Application System	
Hardware or Application System	
Telecommunication	
Source of SoE Attacking Risk of Vulnerabilities: Human	
Key Classes of Component	Rationale of Selection

Knowledge/Skills	
Culture	
Attitude	
Source of SoE Attacking Risk of Vulnerabilities: Process	
Key Classes of Component	Rationale of Selection
Policies and Procedures	
Guidelines	
Legal/law	
Information security Practices	
Source of SoE Attacking Risk of Vulnerabilities: Others	
Key Classes of Component	Rationale of Selection
....	
....	

SAREP: SoE ATTACKING RISK IDENTIFICATION WORKSHEET

SECTION I (ACTIVITY) (SoE ATTACKING RISK OF MANAGEMENT DEFECTS PROFILES)	
Management Defects Profile Name	Please consider how the Management Defects occur? What nature of defects? Whatcaused the defects? Key caned by the defects?Impact?)
Digital Evidence	*(name of digital evidence)*

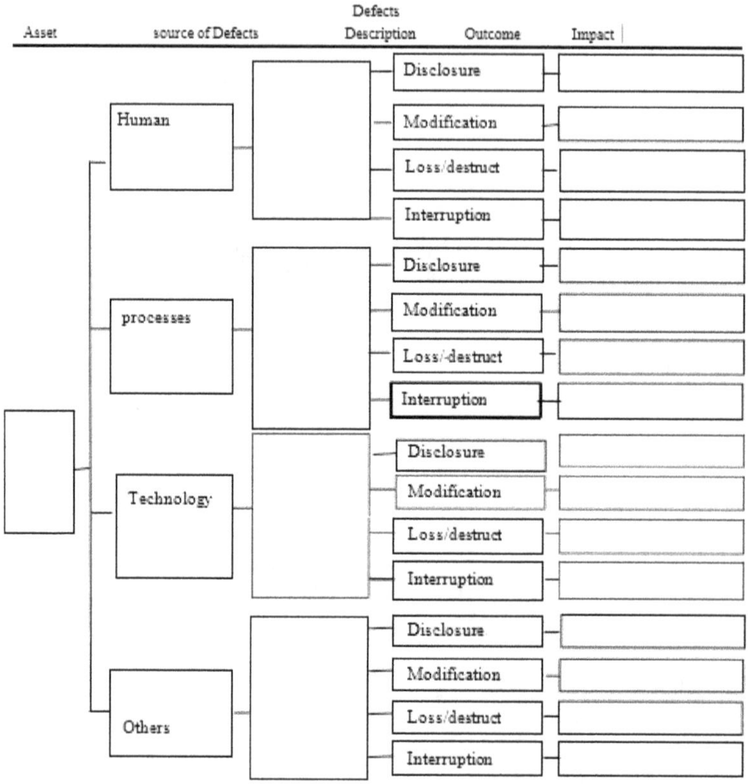

SAREP SoE ATTACKING RISK TREATMENT PLANNING WORKSHEET

SECTION H (ACTIVITY) SoE ATTACKING RISK TREATMENT PLAN WORKSHOP PREPARATION			
Strategic Practices		Organization	ServiceProvider
Protection Strategy	**Security of SoE Attacking Risk Treatment Plan and Training** 1. Maintain/improve the level of SoE Attacking Risk awareness training among staff 2. Sufficient in-house expertise for all supported technology 3. Initiative to improve staff's technology exporting 4. Ensure staff member understand their security roles and responsibility		

	through training, seminar, examination 5. Continues security SoE attacking risk awareness and training programs 6. Organization Member understand their security roles andresponsibilities		
	Security Strategy for SoE attacking risk 1. Incorporate security Consideration into organization's business strategy 2. Security strategy and policies take into consideration the businessstrategy and goal 3. Well documented of the security strategy, goal and objectives 4. Security Strategy related-document widely disseminate relevant staff inthe organization 5. Flexible Security Strategy to adopt unexpected changing environment		
	Security of SoE Attacking Risk Management 1. Make sure secure sufficient fund and resources to conduct information security activities for the prevention technique of SoE attacks 2. Ensure the staff security roles and responsibility defined clearly 3. Make sure consider the SoE Attacking Risk issues when hiring new staff? new service provider 4. Design an effective ways how to manage SoE Attacking Risk 5. Should minimize the communication gap between technology expertise and management regarding to security-related issue		

	Security Policies and Regulations 1. Ensure that organization has comprehensive set of documented, currentsecurity policies regarding SoE attacks 2. Improve the way organization create, updates and communicates security policies 3. Should have procedures to ensure their policies compliance with lawand regulation affecting security 4. Should consistently enforces their security policies 5. Reliable and consistent of security policies and Regulation		
	Collaborative Security Management 1. Should have policies and procedures to protect their information whenworking with external parties. 2. Excellent initiative to protects digital evidence when working with external parties 3. Monitor and verifies that external parties are taking appropriate steps to protect organization's digital evidence. Mutual understanding about security of SoE attacking risk managementand its scope		
	Contingency Planning/Disaster Recovery 1. Should have clearly defined Business Continuity Plan (BCP) 2. BCP should be tested and reliable 3. Make sure that DRP definition/tested BCP well documented and easy toaccess when required 4. Should have clearly defines Date Recovery Plan (DRP) DRP should be tested, workable and reliable		

SAREP SoE ATTACKING RISK TREATMENT PLANNING WORKSHEET

SECTION I (ACTIVITY) DEVELOP INTRGRATION PROTECTION STRATEGY WORKSHEETPROBABILITY EVALUATION CRITERIA WORKSHEET	
PROBABILITY VALUE	FREQUENCY OF OCCORERENCE (SUBJECTIVE)
High	
Medium	
Law	

SECTION J (ACTIVITY B19) DEVELOP INTREGRATED MITIGATION PLAN WORKSHEET		
Outcomes	Probability Description	Probability Measure
Disclosure of Digital Evidence		
Modification of Digital Evidence		
Loss/destruction of a Digital Evidence		
Interruption of Digital Evidence		

SAREP

SoE ATTACKING RISK TREATMENT PLANNING WORKSHEET

SECTION K (ACTIVITY) SoE ATTACKING RISK TRATMENT ACTION LIST			
Operational Practices		Organization	Service Provider
Protection Strategy	**Physical Security** 1. Education and training provided to maintain/improve physicalsecurity practices 2. Sufficient policy and procedures for physical security needs 4. Dedicated personnel responsible for physical security 5. Every staff should responsible for physical security 6. Relevant departments should involve with physical security 7. Physical security requirement clearly understand by InformationSecurity External Expert 8. Physical security requirement verified 9. Physical security plans and procedures for safeguarding the premises. building and any restricted areas are documented andtested 10. Documented policies and procedures created for managing visitor 11. Documented policies and procedures created for physical controlof hardware and software 12. Documented policies and procedures created for controlling physicalaccess to work areas and hardware (computers, communication devices etc and software media 13. Workstation and other components that allow access to sensitiveinformation are physically safeguarded and to prevent unauthorized access 14. Maintenance records are kept to document the repairs andmodifications of facility's physical components		

	15. As individual group's actions with respect to all physicallycontrolled media can be accounted for		
	Organizational Security 1. Education and training provided to maintain improve physicalsecurity practices. 2. Sufficient policy and procedures for Organizational Security 4. Dedicated personnel responsible for Organizational Security 5. Every staff should responsible for Organizational Security 6. Relevant departments should involve with Organizational Security 7. Organizational Security requirement clearly understand byInformation Security External Expert 8. Organizational Security requirement verified 9. Audit and monitoring records are routinely examined for anomaliesand corrective action is taken as needed 10. There are documented and rested security plan (s) for safeguardingthe system and networks 11. Sensitive digital evidence is protected by secure storage (backups stored offsite, discard process for sensitive digital evidence) 12. The integrity of installed software is regularly, verified 13. All system are up to date with respect to revisions, patches,and recommendations in security advisories. 14. There are documented and tested data backup plan for backups or both software and data. All staff understands their responsibilities under the backup plans.		

www.ingramcontent.com/pod-product-compliance
Lightning Source LLC
LaVergne TN
LVHW020414220926
848484LV00018B/2571/J
* 9 7 8 1 6 8 0 5 3 4 2 3 8 *